D1415963

73

These Are the Breaks

These Are the Breaks
a collection of prose

 (3

by Idris Goodwin

Write Bloody Publishing
America's Independent Press

Long Beach, CA

writebloody.com

Goodwin, Idris.
1st edition.
ISBN: 978-1-935904-14-4

Interior Layout by Lea C. Deschenes
Cover Designed by Brett Neiman   http://www.brettneiman.com/
Proofread by Jennifer Roach
Edited by Derrick Brown, shea M gauer, Saadia Byram, Michael Sarnowski
Type set in Aller and Bergamo: www.theleagueofmoveabletype.com

Printed in Tennessee, USA

Write Bloody Publishing
Long Beach, CA
Support Independent Presses
writebloody.com

To contact the author, send an email to writebloody@gmail.com

THESE ARE THE BREAKS

PREFACE

Throughout this book you will hear me refer to myself as black. You will hear me refer to other members of the black race as black. By race I refer to skin color, and by skin color, I mean brown.

Now, commonly brown refers to members of the Latino race (and by race I mean skin color, though in terms of skin color, I mean brown – but not Latino, I mean black). Though it should be noted that Latinos, Indians, Pakistanis, Filipinos, Thai, Vietnamese, Chinese, Japanese, Native Americans, Arabs…pretty much the majority of the world are different variations of the color brown.

But in terms of members of the brown-skinned-black-race, I mean African-American. And by African-American I don't mean like Barack Obama, whose father was born and raised on the continent of Africa and mother was not. We can assume she is the American part. Though Obama is black, not bi-racial.

See, bi-racial typically works best if you're like Chinese and Croatian, or Portuguese and Saudi Arabian. Black means you're not white, and if you're not a nationality then you're black (which means brown, but not Latino). Though it should be noted that many Mexicans, Puerto Ricans, Dominicans, Brazilians, Peruvians, etc., refer to themselves as brown, unless of course they're from Spain. If they're from Spain, brown means gypsy.

When I say black you will surely assume that I am including those from Haiti, Trinidad, Jamaica, Barbados, etc., etc., and I do, in terms of race (skin color). They are black, after all, except of course for those non-black people that live in those countries. But that's an issue of nationality, is it not?

Ok. I am talking about black descendents of stolen Africans who were put on plantations, and later migrated across North and South

America. Not to say that is the quintessential experience of all brown people (by which I mean black, non-Latino-Americans who descended from stolen Africans).

And Afro Latinos you know, black Dominicans like Sammy Sosa[1], or black Puerto Ricans like Roberto Clemente. They are black-brown-black people, and both baseball players. But we'll get to that later.

Culturally speaking, nationally speaking, ethnically speaking, here's what I'm saying: By black I mean brown-skinned Africans and their variants...

No.

By black I mean descendents of stolen people for whom life is a constant improvisation, whose entire rhythm is in constant debate, demand, and duplication. Whose mere existence is an atrocious masterpiece.

By black I mean...

Brown?

---

1   In November 2009 Sammy Sosa showed up at the Latin Grammys with dramatically lightened skin.

1986

The Big Three kept our black shoes shiny. Kept us in dentist chairs reclined. Kept our grins beaming every Christmas morning, action-figure-armed. Lawn mowers, tools, Trans-Ams, T-Birds. All the while the neighborhood watched vigilant.

Some days my brother Malik and I would walk home from school, push open the door, push past magazines and lamps and clothes, everything strewn on the floor. Upstairs and down, a littered mess: a hairdryer, albums, shoes. Minus, of course, the jewelry and electronics.

What's behind door number one? The game had grown familiar. Some mornings as both our parents left for work, Malik and I would spot a young man hunched under a streetlamp. Wonder silent, "Would this be today's contestant?"

They knew us. Kept watch. Hatred escalating. Egg yolks and grape jelly smeared across our living room walls, evidence that our guests were not stealing out of hunger.

We ignored talk of epidemics. Because to be blessed in Detroit in 1986 meant you exercised a daily forgiveness. The house, the cars, the whole lifestyle collapses unless inflated with compassion. You tell yourself the incident was isolated. Hope the man by the streetlamp was merely lost. Hope that when you get home to find the door ajar, he has taken what he needs, pawned it into rock. Hope that you aren't provided the opportunity to talk Reaganomics with him.

In Coleman Young's Motown, you had to face the music, turn your back on the romance. Save yourself.

Meant you had to hear your family ache as you trade the devil you know for the one you don't.

ESHAM

The tape was red. I know that much is certain. We were piled 6 or 7 deep in a Chevy Nova or something like it. Our goofy teenage knees knocking into one another. En route from nowhere to nowhere. Nowhere where we loitered, hoping to be noticed. Though we didn't need to try so hard, pretending like that curfew wasn't ours.

When someone first pulled the red tape from the industry standard stack of rap cassettes, we clowned it. Said it was wack, weak, booty, corny, foul, garbage. OG street hustlers were fine. Smooth Asiatic womanizers got a pass. But we drew the line at devil worship. That was for the heavy metal kids.

But we kept listening, because he said names of streets familiar.

In 1989, rappers came from places like Brooklyn, Queens, Money Earnin' Mount Vernon, South Central, and Compton. But Esham was a rapper from Detroit. His tape read: boomin' words from hell, with an illustration of the classic devil image: horns, forked tail, and a long stringy mustache.

We guffawed. Rewound. Sang along.

Ashy Baptist boys and one Jehovah's Witness, we knew better. But we allowed this 13-year-old, self proclaimed Servant of Satan to acid rap his way into our listless wanderings. Of course, we'd always have church the next morning. Church was 30 miles away in Detroit, just like Esham.

Esham's sound personified the crack era. He was not the manufactured elegance of Berry Gordy's Motown. He was a fetus developed by the Young Boys Incorporated[2] and Coleman Young3[3]. If you listened closely, you could hear the flames. Esham was Devil's Night.

In Detroit, there had always been mischief pre-Halloween: pumpkin flesh, splattered yolks, doorbells. Dare devils giving their angels the night off. But over time, the gas became fume. Pipelines spilled heroin, hollowing homes. Moltov cocktails replaced rolls of toilet paper. Devil's Night was scarier than Halloween.

In 1984, more than 800 fires branded the city dangerous. Smoke blanketed the sky black as affluent brown folk took white flight out of town. Headed straight to booming suburbs, moving trucks subsidized by the auto companies. We, too, made the exodus to medicated environs.

Together with other transplanted black boys, my brother and I piled in the Ford Festiva, anxious for escape. We blasted Esham, howled devilish laughter as we raced through the sleepy streets, the same streets that saved us from all we fetishized. The wicked voice, the pulse, the Pistons, the boomin' sounds of our birthplace.

---

2   An African American Drug Cartel operating primarily out of Detroit in the late 1970's through the 1980's

3   The first African American mayor of Detroit. 1974-1993

RESPONSE #1

On February 21st, 2010, the east wall of the Art Institute of Chicago's New Modern Wing was defaced with a fifty-foot graffiti piece painted by a team of writers in about 20 minutes.

On March 10th, a graffiti writer named SOLE was painting a mural on the wall of an abandoned factory. When police showed up and gave chase, he flung himself into the Chicago River and drowned.

> *"We began shocking common sense, public opinion, education, institutions, museums, good taste, in short the whole prevailing order"*
> —The Dada Manifesto, 1918

> *"Dada philosophy is the sickest, most paralyzing and most destructive thing that has ever originated from the brain of man"*
> —American Art News, 1918

So somebody went and done drew a mustache on the Mona Lisa. Which is to say, somebody took aerosol to staple, mocked how we consume our culture. I imagine them smiling when they did it. Because it's all just make believe, isn't it? Private space // public space. Unreal lines. Agreed upon modes of presentation.

The image has long since been blasted away. It's business as usual at The Art Institute of Chicago: Euro

centrism and expensive cheese shoved down throats that reflux the same tired conversations.

Law abiding artists, civilized, pontificate: What does it mean? Building upon the legend, filling up temporary space. Is it: Vandalism? Street Art? Graffiti? Whatever it is has proven gatekeepers ignorant by infiltrating the institutional art machine.

Terms like "hip-hop" woo corporate philanthropists, "urban" a call to arms for chic intelligentsia the world over. It's widely emulated. Detroit, Michigan. Iowa City, Iowa. Those same bubble letters, jutting angles. Santa Fe, New Mexico. Cheyenne, Wyoming. Those same stencils and polemic sentiment. Nairobi, Kenya. Amman, Jordan.

I am a rapper introduced to hip-hop culture through commodity. My early engagements with rap music were mediated by radio, cable television, the sterilized confines of the mall's record chain. I experienced the renegade of rap after it had been scrubbed, bleeped. I felt the furious wild style from a safe distance, witnessed the body's pops and spins behind glass. I copied.

I, like many artists, have benefited from those who risked their bodies crossing invented boundaries. Those who risk their bodies to steal, hustle, con, bend the bars to prove another paradigm is possible. We pick and tear, wear their skin, swallow their tongues to better define ourselves. We press their remains on t-shirts long after they've been crushed by narrow, elitist agendas.

It's all make believe. Institutes are machinations like constructs of race, wealth, success. A shared hallucination. All that is real and undeniable is this animal need to survive, the human desire to exist after the flesh dissolves.

There will always be those who loiter outside our hallowed halls, those who haven't a taste for stinky cheese. And if they are not greeted, they will introduce themselves.

It will not be creased nor presentable. It will test the patience of the liberal and learned. We will have to stop for a moment, mute ourselves, and think about what it really means.

OLD LADIES AND DOPE BOYS

I.

Behind doors with multiple locks, old ladies sit silent, their GI bill homes kept from fading by green gardens and fresh paint. They sit silent, artifact-surrounded, memory thick: skinned knees, rock heads, uncles, sweaters and aprons floured. Framed photos of Dr. King, military uniforms, perfect afros, graduation caps, S-curls, dashikis, Brooks Brothers and Cross Colours. Archived on the shelf: Ebony, Essence, Black Enterprise, Jet. The engraved King James Bible next to the 10th Edition New World Revised Bible next to the pocket-sized Bible. Some spare in the drawer.

When you come home from global visions, they get a ride to the grocery store across town. The good one. The bus stopped running here in the 1980's. They cook for you, just you, a full family meal, hoping the aroma will lure. Then maybe the leaf can be slid through dining room table.

II.

Across the street, the whole family razor blades and triple fades, fitted caps stooping over triple beams and mayonnaise jars. Baking soda water boils. Once it hardens, they chop.

Neighbors morph into ghosts, into shreds, while the talented tenth look ahead like Lot.

III.

Detroit blocks. Old ladies and dope boys standoff on porches, unafraid. Neither buying what the other is selling.

HIP HOP ON ADAMS ROAD

Van Hoosen Middle School was about a mile from my home and I'd walk. Sometimes my friend Jason would walk with me. Walking. Talking. Turned to popping turned to spitting. Then the spits went round and round, lips exploding. His whole body jumped.

Jason had discovered beat boxing. Sloppily, but he'd deciphered the code.

When Jason and I first met, he was Megadeth, Iron Maiden, Guns N Roses. I was Run Dmc, the Fat Boys, LL Cool J, Eazy E. Now here was Jason playing air drums with his mouth, motioning for me to join in.

"Make up your own rhymes," he said, and so I gave it a shot. Elementary at first, Dr. Seuss style. Hat, fat, cat. Two pre-teen boys throwing arms into high motion, a concert of spit and rhyme up Adams Road. Jason's face a bright red as confused cars inched by.

In the weeks that followed, Jason broke out his Yamaha electronic drum pad in attempt to duplicate his body's music, the kind that erupted from his mouth. But it wasn't the same. The beats he tapped with sticks lacked the round warmth of lungs, the authenticity of breath and skin. Next, we tried my Casiotone keyboard. The built-in microphone allowed for a few seconds of voice recording. We jammed the sun to sleep.

Day after day, we meandered through textbooks. Ate canned fish and defrosted green beans. Watched sitcoms. All the while, we thought about tomorrow's walk, and the day after that. Unable to sleep, brains beating out the rhythm of possibility.

VINYL

"As fine as it is, it can still be made better."
-*Thomas Edison*

"It's sort of like a big pile of broken dreams. If you're making records, you're adding to this pile whether you want to admit it or not."
—*DJ Shadow on digging for used records*

There's no question about it. They're no good for the environment. Vinyl is petroleum-based, after all. To manufacture records requires heavy hydraulic equipment, chemical baths, aerosol, and electricity. The lacquer is married to metal by electric shock. Then the two are separated. The mother is stored while the metal father stamps each son unique. Every press and cut slightly different by the tiniest increment of space. A record is a negotiation of space, of thought, of hands, the oils absorbed to bone. No, they're not cost effective.

They're not portable, either. Most people can't even play records at home because, professional DJs aside, who owns a record player anymore? Some nostalgic enthusiasts, maybe, and aging relatives who perpetually postpone their garage sales.

Vinyl dominated recorded sound for almost a century. It makes absolutely no sense to continue creating records. And yet that's precisely what makes them so poetic.

You form a relationship with your vinyl. You must handle them with caution. You must dust them, cradle them into record player, then sit and listen. Look at the image on the cardboard cover. Read and re-read the liner notes. You do not take records with you to the gym. They are not portable background filler meant to ease your isolation.

The digital avenue is clean, intangible, impersonal. My iPod Shuffle continues to astound people with its utter compactness, considering it can hold around 120 songs. But it's just not the same. Digital music lacks vibration. It's a series of numbers standing in for calloused fingertips, human hands that loop and reloop, hoping for the one right take. It's sound approximated, which is why the files are so easy to steal.

Detroit's Archer Record Pressing factory is the last of its kind. As Motor City struggles to pheonix, Archer Record's archaic machines rear to life, thanks to kids who defied their parent's instructions to keep their hands off the vinyl. They are poetic, vinyl records, precisely because they are made in factories like Archer. Or URP in Nashville. Or VFM in Middlesex. Records made by folks who inspect, then discard, 50 percent of the output due to imperfections. Some of these employees have made records for decades. They pass down stories of the executives from Motown and Stax sleeping in the apartment above the factory on trips through town. "Wayne Newton played a show up here after he put out his first record," they say of the factory. "Hank Williams celebrated his 68th birthday here," they say of the factory. It's this sort of inherited legendry, played from the well-worn grooves of factory men and women, that keeps record enthusiasts beholden to their craft. Despite digital, they keep pressing down and pushing on.

We all know the inevitable futures of people who work in factories. After time, they become theoretical. Transform themselves into digital, into a static series of numbers. It's no surprise, then, that by the end of the Regan administration, on the precipice of Bush senior, compact discs surpassed vinyl sales. The same year the Soviets left Afghanistan, a year after my family left Detroit, the corporate squeeze forced record stores to order more plastic. The sort of plastic produced by foreign technology. Cheap plastic, encoded. There is nothing poetic about lasers deciphering numbers. That's the stuff of science fiction, another Asimov paperback.

And yet, 20 years later, stores like the Record Collector in Iowa City, Homers in Omaha, Gramaphone in Chicago, keep their crates filled with records, a gallery of sound art. True school DJ's keep their fingers on the grooves. Lovers of the pop and crackle, that old, deep-rooted vibration, search bin after bin for familiar names. Seek out that communal experience that transports them from home into a world of sonic history.

When this is all over — when we're nothing more than dust on rock — remnants of our civilization will slump, mute. New settlers will sort through our piles of broken dreams. And vinyl records, they will project the sound of our humanity, will prove that we carved sound into objects, felt music the way a number never could, because the groove was real and we were once real, too.

THESE ARE THE BREAKS

You've heard the myths and legends. 70's south Bronx. Poly-culture pot of gold, echo urban stomps. Hands releasing ratchets to touch the vinyl, stroke the grooves. Nodding back and forth like wrist that found new ways to prove. And show, and grow, and blend. Bring it back again. Edit. Gut. And tear new names up out the wind.

You've heard about criminal. The daring, death-defying so-called underground. So-called urban styling. With the Asian technology that flooded the colony. Bytes of info, bit and flip.

Tools inverted. Sound stolen and distorted like legislation imported. Stolen like real estate, inventions and credit. Broken like neighborhoods when interstates arrive.

So the children of the losing war, they built a bridge again. Pulse to pulse catapults, lasso pulling different folks on subway cars, on foot or spokes called Philosophical. Diasporic.

The magical mining through mud for the fantastical. Celebrating. Chanting out: Raw, strike, flame ignite. Heart, livid, never break for the night.

For blocks and blocks, hips-head. Let the Breakers break. The stale left dead.

Yes,
we ex
plode
on the
break is the place where the poem get laced. Let the rhythm hit us
first in the face.

And,

in bet
ween,
all these
bangs and the bumps and the pows and the thumps, we explore
time's signature, we can't get enough.

And,
to this
day,
the words we
say been influenced by the molding of music, changing it around for
a brand new usage.

Now Bird riding horse with Bach. So-called third world pulled into
the concerto. Some wanna cap, regulate madness. Scared of the
beautiful mescegenated scratches. But they never die down, they only
get liver. Can't nobody copyright fire. Can't nobody copyright fire.
Can't nobody copyright fire.

'Cause it's spreadin' like it always do. Suburban, urban, and the rural,
too. Plugged in. Tucked in.

Finding new ways to tune in. Finding new ways to stand up. Speak
out. Get by. Finding new ways to say how long you been here.
Finding new ways to stop the erasure of markings.

Breaking down all the talking, coded, loaded, locked and smoking,
stocked. Because it be about the body, the body's reaction. The
lungs, throat, tongue. The limbs rebellion.

Finding new ways to break the rhythm expected. Finding new ways
to break the laws of stolen land.

And some, they like to say they got patents on the noise. Numbers
on the invisible, barcodes on light. But fire, you can't copy, right?

THE FLAVOR UNIT

The landscape had changed, sure, but Mom was determined that we kids wouldn't fade. She and other suburban black moms from the neighborhood united their children in hopes that our presence en mass might deflect the assimilating influence of the white majority. The imperative was clear: we had to stay black.

To the Rochester Hills Public Library staff, it must have looked like a lunar eclipse ascended on that Saturday afternoon. All those hi-top sneakers and haircuts, mama jokes and mother land medallions. Most of our parents represented Detroit, Pontiac, Flint and Saginaw. Some of the moms had West Indian, and African accents, though their kids spoke the same '88 Ebonics we'd all adopted. At least, around one another. Especially around one another.

Yo! MTV Raps had just debuted and we were all hip to it. Naturally the ice was broken as we threw and caught references with glee.

We called ourselves the Flavor Unit, a name lifted from a prominent East Coast consortium of our favorite rappers.[4] It was fitting, as we thought of ourselves as lively, bright, colorful, bursting with panache.

Puffing our personalities to volume 10.

At the meeting, we threw out big ideas. We'd get t-shirts; red, black and green of course, like X Clan.

We'd start a newsletter. Plan a series of outings and events. A Christmas — Kwannza party.

The t-shirts did in fact arrive, but our more ambitious plans failed

---

4   The Flavor Unit was comprised of such notables as Queen Latifah, D Nice, Black Sheep, Naughty By Nature, and Freddie Foxxx. To my knowledge, they were unaware of the Rochester Hills branch.

to actualize. Knowing of one another's existence proved satisfaction enough, sans newsletter. Naturally, the Flavor Unit splintered into generic high school factions: the cool with the cool, the jocks with jocks, the criminal-minded with the criminal-minded, and so on. We were nothing more than a microcosm of a microcosm. Aware but ultimately strangers to one another, unwilling to turn down our adolescent noise long enough to make out what our hearts were screaming.

Some years later our group had an unofficial reunion. Every year, college recruiters from historically black colleges would assemble in Detroit. Under pressure from our high school's only black teacher, our vice principal rented a fifteen-passenger van for a Flavor Unit fieldtrip.

It was undeniable that we'd ignored one another over the years. Or else we'd called each other out for playing the wrong side when it mattered. But now, crammed together in such a small space, outnumbering our own vice-principal, we softened. Breathed a little easier. Tossed and caught references again with ease, broke down black sci-fi and gangster rap. Spent the day dreaming of what our futures could look like. "Why didn't we do this more often?" we asked one another.

Upon our return, the vice-principal, quiet the entire trip, thanked us for teaching him so much. But once that mobile classroom settled to stall, it was never the same again. Back in Rochester Hills, back to black moms and white friends. Declaring our individuality whilst locking ourselves into one deep breadth.

SOMETHING ABOUT LYING

Most performers will tell you that no matter how many hours they've chalked up on stage, there's always a feeling that one day the audience will turn on you. One day someone will rise from seat and yell, "He's a fake! A phony! Put him on the rail!"

I had been doing plays on a twig and twist-tie budget for a couple years, which, at its best, got me ripped apart in the local press. My favorite: "In Goodwin's latest play, a character repeats, 'Don't tell me what I need!' Well, it's the opinion of this humble reviewer that Goodwin, you need a rewrite."

I was 26, had just graduated from the Art Institute of Chicago with a Masters in the Fine Art of Writing, which meant that I was sleeping on a mattress in my friend's unheated art studio. Somehow I managed to land a job interview at the progressive Perspectives Charter School. They were looking for an 8th grade Speech and Drama teacher.

The interview team asked about my approach to discipline. "I'll employ any form of discipline you want," I said. "Dunce caps, eraser slapping, public ridicule. I'm a company man."

I had done some teaching before, mostly a mixed bag of teen writing workshops. I was well accustomed to the ambitious, dreamy young artists who gazed out the window in deep contemplation. I was also well accustomed to wearing my pajamas 'till noon. But the Perspectives job, it was a daily affair. I had to set an alarm clock, look presentable, carry myself with a modicum of decency. I had to create actual curricula around tangible goals. The kids I'd be teaching, they were like most of us in 8th grade: looking for any excuse to drive our teachers toward the anti-depressants. It would be a small price to pay, though. I needed socks without holes.

Teaching is the ultimate performance for an audience who would rather be elsewhere. Day one, I stood before twenty blue-uniformed, blank brown faces. Girls whose hair was pressed into colorful barrettes and boys whose shirttails hung sloppily from their trousers. I watched them watching me, judging me, sharpening their ridicule, just waiting for me to crack. But I wasn't gonna crack. I over-planned and overexplained, improvised and diverted. Some days I just threw silent hail Marys into the ether and crossed my fingers. I never let them see me sweat, even when the classroom was clearly on fire.

My main fire-starter was Michael Young, the resident wise-ass. He had this young Fresh Prince thing that appeared to be working very well for him. Except with me, because after all, that's my shtick. I had to show this upstart that he couldn't encroach on my charming troublemaker terrain. So I was a little tougher on Michael than some of the other students, but only by a bit. I liked to knock him off his self-appointed Fonzerelli pedestal, much to the joy of the other students, who were often eclipsed by Michael's swagger. My ability to steal Michael's thunder helped me to build trust with the class.

The weeks began to pass a little quicker, the classes a little smoother. But then, it happened. Michael caught me slipping. "Where's my pen, Mr. Goodwin?" he asked. "What pen?" I said, distracted. "You didn't have a pen yesterday, so I loaned you mine. It was my favorite pen and you said you'd give it back.

Where's my pen?" I shook my head slowly, shifted my feet. "Give it back?" I said. "I thought I gave it back."

Did I take Michael's pen? Probably, but I don't remember. I certainly looked for it, in the classroom, in my car, in my apartment. Day after day, Michael would ask, loudly so that the whole class could hear, "Mr. Goodwin, where is my pen?" And day after day I told him, "I don't have it. I gave it back to you."

The class began to split on the great debate: Mr. Goodwin, Thief or Cool Teacher Guy with Wrinkled Clothes? The most loyal of the bunch came to my aide, but other students questioned with big, innocent pre-teen eyes. Slowly, Michael regained his thunder. I had morphed into the oppressor, a lying reviser of history, another authoritative adult bully, petty and irresponsible.

During the last week of the program, I was forced to discipline Michael for some silly 8th grade crime, like pulling hair or kicking a trashcan. Administration called Michael's father to the school, and guess who had to face him? That's right, not my understudy.

Michael's father was as you might imagine him, an imposing fellow with hands that could strangle a yak. Despite his icy demeanor, I could tell that Papa Young was annoyed to be pulled from work to pick up his knucklehead son, just like my own imposing yak-strangling father when Van Hoosen Middle School called to report my witticisms and antics.

Michael sat at his father's side looking up at me, terrified. I knew that look well. It was the look of impending doom. The look of gazelles when they hear a rustle in the distance.

Mr. Young asked me in a cold, low voice, "So, what'd he do?" Michael's desperate eyes locked on me as I formulated my answer.

I couldn't send a fellow entertainer to the chair just for experimenting with his craft. Michael was merely a frustrated social commentator using his natural gifts to sway popular opinion. He probably didn't get much attention from his dad, just a laundry list of restrictions and punishments. So what if Michael used my class as a venue for his creative development?

"Nothing too bad, Mr. Young," I said. "We were doing some improv and it got a little carried away. Michael is a very committed performer, he just needs to exercise some better judgment."

I looked at Michael and shrugged as if to say, "Best I can do for ya, kid. You'll be remembered." Michael smiled back. It was more a smirk than a smile. He looked up at his father and said, "This is the guy I told you about, dad. The one who stole my pen."

WHAT I LEARNED FROM AL JOLSON

It was the 8th grade, maybe the 7th. I was sleeping over at Jason's house. It was a Friday night and we were competing to see who could stay up the latest. Watching Robocop in the family room with his dad. We were lightweights, fell asleep maybe an hour into the movie.

Sometime later I woke up. Refocused my eyes. Robocop had ended and now the screen was smeared with high contrast: white man, burnt black cork. His cheeks, his chin, his eyes, his forehead, smothered. I shuddered, confused and fearful of this two-toned Boogieman, three-piece suit and creepy smile. The Elvis of the genre, here was the first man to be audible in a motion picture.

I turned and saw that Jason's dad was watching closely, inquisitively. He glanced down at me. Realized that I was awake. But he couldn't change the channel, because if he changed the channel then he would draw attention to the fact that he was watching a documentary on Al Jolson. So instead he left it on, pretending that he was not watching a documentary on Al Jolson.

These were the days before cultural sensitivity.

Maybe 25 minutes into the documentary — an overview of Jolson's biography, his penchant for smearing black stuff on his face before singing — Jason's dad said, "You know, It's just what people did in those times." I had been taught to respect my elders, especially when eating at their table, which I had done on many nights previous. So I just nodded. Pretended to go back to sleep, Jolson crooning Swanne in my dreams.

The next day my mother asked about the sleepover. I told her we ate pizza, drank Pepsi, watched an hour of Robocop, then a documentary about Al Jolson. "You know, It's just what people did in those times," I said.

She didn't respond, not even a word. She just stared at me. It was a different sort of stare, not mother to son, not anything I had the life experience to decipher. Looking back, I see in her face the inexplicable sting of betrayal. The line between adult and child was simple no longer.

When it is my turn I wonder if I will change the channel. Or will we watch quietly and just let the man sing his song?

BLACK FACE ALONG
THE GREAT WHITE WAY

There has been another incident.

The radio host is taking calls regarding this reoccurring compulsion of those lighter than brown. A feeble voice explains that growing up in the Midwest, she remembers the productions. Though she repeats they were all in good fun, she could certainly understand why the African-American community was upset.

"It's an old theatrical tradition."
—Bojangles Robinson in defense of black face

When I was growing up, if somebody called you an Uncle Tom, it meant you were suckin' up to the white man. This was the penultimate put down. If somebody called you an Unlce Tom, your heart would sink to hell. I expended great energy ducking that phrase, steering clear of coming off anywhere close. That is, until I learned about its origin.

Abolitionist writer Harriet Beacher Stowe wrote the novel *Uncle Tom's Cabin* in 1852 as a response to the Fugitive Slave Act, which had passed just two years earlier.[5] She sought to expose the savage horrors of slavery. In her novel, Uncle Tom is a long-suffering, martyr character who dies so that others may have freedom. *Uncle Tom's Cabin* became the best-selling novel of the 19th century.

The traveling theatrical Minstrel show was the dominant populist form of the day so naturally Stowe's novel was quickly adapted. Scriptwriters reinterpreted the novel, removing all anti-slavery

---

5   Under this act, if a slave escaped past the Mason Dixon line into a slavery-free zone, his or her master reserved the right to reclaim him or her.

sentiment, instead transforming the text into a gallery of caricature. Uncle Tom himself became a shiftless, weak, asexual buffoon. Not surprisingly, a white man wearing burnt cork portrayed the character on stage. White actors gallivanted as all of the black characters in *Uncle Tom's Cabin*. It is this white-black-buffoon, this Hollywood-stained Uncle Tom, that black folks won't go anywhere near.

True, Stowe's book had an impact on our literary culture, but it was public access compared to the CNN that was the traveling minstrel show.

Advancements in filmmaking technology only served to enhance minstrel's legacy. *Birth of a Nation*, the first major full-length motion picture that defined filmmaking standards, showcased white men in black face.

It's said that the last full-scale minstrel productions were performed in the late 1950s, but their tenacious spirit has yet to die. In this new century, minstrel shows set up shop at college parties throughout the United States.

January 2007:

Students at Clemson University in South Carolina celebrated Martin Luther King Jr.'s legacy by dressing in black face and fake tattooing their bodies with the phrase *thug life*. "We just wanted a gangsta party for fun," the Clemson students said. "You know, like the hip hop culture. So we dressed up."

A few states west, students at Tarleton University in Texas throw an identical party. Black face. Dew rags. Aunt Jemima costumes. One kid wears a shirt that reads, *I Love Chicken*.

A few states northeast, at Connecticut Law School, graduate students respond to Martin Luther King Jr.'s cultural contribution by getting drunk and emulating images perpetuated in music videos. They pose in black face, waving plastic guns, flashing mean mugs and fake gold teeth.

October 2007:

Louisiana College students make a video for internet distribution. They're at the beach smearing mud on themselves. Claiming to be the Jena 6.

Novemeber 2008:

A Northwestern University PhD student blackens up to play Jamaican Hussein Bolt.

January 2009:

At Macalester College in Saint Paul, Minnesota, a white student dressed as a Ku Klux Klan member held a noose wrapped around the neck of a white kid in black face.

May 11, 2010:

A student at Bethel University blacks up to impersonate Lil' Wayne.

No doubt there will be another incident this Halloween at a campus near you.

In photos, these college kids look wholesome, healthy, bright, all-American. They will likely evolve into lawyers and principals, police officers and politicians. The teachers of tomorrow. "We didn't know it would offend so many people," America's children respond when the photos leak, followed by a few flimsy apologies. "It's not like we don't have black friends," they say, though there are no (actual) black students photographed. Not that it would make a difference. Even black folk participated in minstrel shows, dressed in black face the same as white actors. They were considered the Uncle Toms, the sellouts.

One-dimensional robes easily donned then discarded. Pimps, hoes, gangstas, sellouts, oreos.

Whose imagination is being enacted?

THE HEADBANGER

A hybrid junkyard. A post-industrial apocalypse. A bombed-out Hooverville infested with puffy black shadows, men armed like a 70's street gang. This is a music video.

There are pipes, chains. One guy grips an oversized mallet like he's testing his strength at a carnival. Another guy swings a scythe, but no wheat grows in this graffiti-ed purgatory.

The music video, it's called The Headbanger, but it's a far cry from feathered blond hair, tight pants, and double neck Les Paul guitars.

Its 1992 and hip-hop music has just split its hammer pants. I'm 14 and I study this music video almost every day.

Spotlights zip the screen, helicopters flashing intermittent reveals: whites of eyes, black ski masks, frantic spit, panting breath, those long stare downs, dead serious.

Someone yells, "Yo where's my hoodie? I want to get wild and cause some ruckas!"

EPMD was my favorite group. The Headbanger is from their 4th album. It's a classic posse record, a collaboration of the group's core members, Erick Sermon and Parrish Smith, plus featured appearances by K Solo and Redman. The quartet calls themselves the Hit Squad.

The object of a posse record is to out-style, out-brag, out-skill your fellow rappers. In the hierarchy of posse cuts, the opening and closing of the song rate as the most highly coveted spots. To go first made you the boatman, safely carrying the listener into the song. To go last? That made you the rapper with the wildest style. The song's nearly over, after all, and three other rappers have tried convincing the listener that they're the best. The final voice must overshadow all that's come before.

It's those first and final lines of a posse record that go on to define it. On the Scenario, it's Phife Dawg first and Busta Rhymes last. On the Symphony, it's Masta Ace first and Big Daddy Kane last. Say these lines in a circle of hip hop fans and watch for the shift in posture.

The Headbanger is one of those rare posse records in which the first and last words are given to the same person. In this case, Redman. His verse is littered with trademark perversity, hubris, and non-sequiturs. And the lines that earn him the key to Posse Cut City, they're exemplary of the compromise every rap fan makes regarding the First Amendment. Because real hip-hop was unwavering, brash, rugged, "hardcore no R&B singer."

I was a teenage boy searching for the right armor. I wanted to don the grim reaper garb and live in the Headbanger video. Project wicked couplets at the camera. It wasn't such a far off fantasy. The Headbanger video could've been shot anywhere in Detroit's vacant cityscape, the Detroit we drove through once a week. Back home, tucked away in well-lit suburban Michigan, it was clean trimmed haircuts, freshly cut grass, streamlines, and Christianity.

But the Hit Squad, they dressed like hell's construction workers: black Carhartt jackets, thick-soled work boots, vests, wool hats.

In the video someone hollers, "I'm the original rap criminal!" Fingers mime trigger pull. To an uninformed viewer, this might be cause for alarm, but I wanted in.

It's 1992. "Represent" and "Real Hip Hop" are the words of the day, punching holes in the ivory pedestal, snorting residue from scud missiles. Dr. Dre's The Chronic murdered any sense of sensitivity the genre had to offer.

No room for clown princes, smooth new jack swing, women. Only nocturnal mobs posing for the camera, threatening the ghost army of wack MCs and too-soft men.

Every day around 4, I'd watch the Hit Squad. Here was a world without rivers. No budding flowers, no white kids asking to feel your hair, no questions of future. Here, a principal might catch a beat down, but a dope MC would get his name aerosoled onto a concrete pillar.

This stylized vision of urban rebellion had me refashioning myself baggy, rugged, draped in Construction clothes, looking for a jackhammer. I dressed like I was ready to put out a hit. Every morning in the mirror asking myself, *am I ready to get real?*

SIGNAL: A MOTHER-SHIP SONG

When it rainstorm, when it thunder, he imagine under blankets.
Flashlight-handed, comic books, dramatic action. Head clouds and
rainbows, puddles, critters under moon-glow. The wind kicks like a
bass drum, out the window he's careening.

On his mission, already soaked. Lands in the backyard, barefoot and
cold.

Tonight he's making contact. Tonight he'll make the contact.
Tonight he'll make, tonight he'll make, tonight he'll make the
contact with that super sonic, so divine. Socializing, otherworldly to
rescue him.

Will they send down praise and ladders, praise and ladders, praise and
ladders? Or will they send down black adders? Praise and ladders,
praise and ladders.

So the wind, it kicks up once again. Lighting claws the midnight
canvas, but he's not scared, he done this before. Every time the sky
gets raw, he's super-rappin' to the blackness swirling around him. He
starts snapping, cracking language, twisting verbiage, reinvention.
Reality redefinition, sanity heighten, sensor to reshape. He reports
and makes mistakes.

This aint the poetry that he got taught. He let go those computer
thoughts. Strange language, all coded. Who he fought, who he stole,
and what blood he want spilled in milk, who got the heart all locked
and rusted. Those traditions weighed heavy. That nervous hand, that
aint ready.

The weather angry just like him, but rain can't wash the sting from
skin. So he keep rappin', trying to connect with those alien folks that
love that wreck. He keep rappin', trying to connect with those alien

folks that love that wreck.

He purge the shackle, purge the sports. Purge the cartoon, purge the ghost. He purge the channels, purge the shoes. Purge the brown bag, purge the blues.

The drops are anvils smash his eyes. He stay open, just trying to get open.

Signal, signal, send a signal. He sends a signal in the storm.

Will he connect? Will he connect? Through screams and razors out his lungs, will he connect? Will he connect?

Signal, signal, send a signal. He sends a signal in the storm.

DON'T BE A SELLOUT

"He aint talkin' 'bout me," you say when the song comes up.

Everyone agrees; Death Certificate is Ice Cube's best. But this song, True to the Game, makes you cringe:

Soon as y'all get some dough / Ya wanna put a white b**** on your elbow.

You conjure their razor blade stares, the teeth-sucking, neck-craning black girls who you're not dating. No, your girlfriend is white. White like your ex-girlfriend and your next girlfriend. White like the girls on 90210.

You, you wanna be white and corny.

Your white buddies wear t-shirts that say Anthrax, Dead Kennedys, Black Flag, and Faith No More, bands you secretly enjoy. They have drum sets in their basements, all the premium cable channels. They have four times as many comic books as you do. They swear in front of their parents, call them Jack and Nancy, Robert and Fran, Larry and Shirley. A lifestyle you secretly desire.

Get the hell out! Stop being an Uncle Tom, you little sell-out.

You still go to church in Detroit, that has to be worth something. You tithe, 10 percent of your lawn cutting money. You listen to hip-hop music, can rattle off the lyrics. You throw away your Mc Hammer tape, your INXS tape, your skateboard. You can't be a sellout.

Stop selling out your race and wipe that stupid-ass smile off your face.

To make friends you do impressions of Eddie Murphy doing impressions of Bill Cosby. Shuck, jive, strut.

You sag, tilt, lean, chop off the "g's" and "er's", stretch yourself hard not to talk proper. Your father is eloquent. Your brother is an ice cube. But you, you feel white and corny. A punching bag hangs in your basement. You wrap your hands tight, put on headphones. Beat yourself into submission.

A message to the Oreo cookie: find a mirror and take a look, G. Do you like what you see?

You study your reflection. You're dressed like Ice Cube in the video, all black on the outside. You can't be a sellout, you tell yourself. You came from people who were sold.

You ain't white, so stop holding your ass tight.

You stop saying "like" so much. Tell people in Rochester that you're from Detroit. Tell people in Detroit you live near Pontiac, right down the block from danger.

Your father takes an interest in golf. He buys you a bag so that you will join him. It is the last place you want to be on a Saturday because you're 15 and trying so hard to stay true to the game. Your father wants to teach you how to play through the rough. You whine. You scoff. You hope for a thunderstorm.

The bag sits in the garage untouched. You'd rather spend your time practicing your mean mug. Aint a damn thing funny.

Get a grip Oreo and be true to the game.

You move to Chicago. Here, you can breathe a bit easier. You're in a black-approved city, even though your crew is the same pale complexion they've always been.

You're at a party. You overhear a guy, the one with the chin stud from Minneapolis, the DJ with whom you talk records from time to time. He's chatting to some other guy in ratty dreads and giant pants. "*That kid*," he says about you, "is whiter than I am." You wonder if he culls his criteria from the records in his crate. The sounds, the cover poses, the drug-induced imaginings.

When white kids get into hip-hop, it's a phase they're going through. When black kids lack the accoutrement, then they are dubbed sellouts. And you can't be a sellout, because that shit don't sell.

EXODUS

My dad's mother is a well traveled gust of Georgia pecan air. The oldest living relative with a Detroit zip code. Five of her seven children made a reverse exodus to reclaim the same southern United States that once owned our ancestors. "Mama, you need to move down here with us." Their subtle suggestions escalated to a united demand, piercing her stubborn exterior.

"The city is broke," she says of Detroit. She will let go of the southeast side house on Annabelle St. and move to the college town of Athens, GA. I imagine her in a U of G bulldogs jacket, hanging out in the quad, talking Fanon philosophy. She is grateful and southern about her predicament but the playwright in me thirsts for subtext and the poet is drunk on the romance of her journey home after a courageous migration towards prosperity. "There is nothing there, Dris. 'cept some red dirt and a one room church," she says of the family land in Stovall, GA. "But you'll be living in Athens," I remind her, "and not too far from Atlanta." But she knows this and much more than my limited scope can comprehend.

I trade addresses with the frequency of seasons. I forget that there is something about a house. The stories that dent walls. Voices that topple ceramic lamps. Authentic black sounds dancing from basement to the attic. Chicken pox treated. Switches broken from trees and marched painfully inside. Television trays loaded with corn bread bricks and pig. My grandfather's husky laugh and razor wit are embedded deep within the layers of paint. It was right there on Annabelle St. where my grandparents provided life. Perhaps (and most likely) the poet in me is doing more than he needs. Maybe she is just too damn tired to sort through and dispose of decades.

THE SOUTH LOOP

The derelicts' serenade smelled like midnight. Lips cracked from 151 and Grapefruit juice, they sang their pleas into starless sky. Prayed for Harold Washington's return. Ashy fingers pointed to temple, hands tethered to brown-papered bottles like so many burlap sandbags. Their sanctuary: a brick wall, a bulletproofed hot dog stand, the burnt burgundy Hotel Roosevelt, that transient den where a woman once threw herself from a 12th story window.

I arrived a few days before my 19th birthday. Six hundred square feet and a futon to my name. Sirens, security guards, bright lights, blind awakening. The closest grocery store was 6 blocks away and I was broke anyway. Cigarettes only cost $1.90.

For nourishment, I would venture on red and orange lines. I'd drift late, dodge her calls. Most nights bent over sinks, toilets. Grant Park sleepless, huddled under fog. Without friends, I lost the sound of my voice.

More than a decade later, a glossy, digitalized South Loop. Derelicts long ago drowned out by stroller squeak, dog bark, bicycle chatter. A green orb rotating: gas, gas, gas. Dry cleaners and coffee shops and clean swept balconies. Thai restaurants with French names. The rattle of the orange elevated car a baseline to condo construction.

Though dressed like a mall, underneath I can still taste the chaos, hear the desperate, curdling howl dragged across wind, relentless.

This, my port of entry, my first impression, my ten year home, a Polaroid slow to develop.

ME AND MAHMOUD
DOWN BY THE DEAD SEA

Summer 2006, the warmest summer in 350 years. The 24-hour news machine delights in beheadings, honor killings, suicide bombings, armed Arabs demanding justice via grainy video footage.

Terrorists burn into my consciousness. I imagine myself flanked by bearded men.

The irony, of course, is that I'm a hip-hop documentary filmmaker assigned to the Middle East to deconstruct Arab stereotypes. A left leaning advocate of social justice, yet I'm terrified of winding up like so many American journalists who venture into the region.

Day one in Amman, Jordan. The hospitality's warm, the August sun warmer. My crew and I interview folks who devote their lives to calming the region's fires, yet I can't stop mapping exit strategies in every building we enter.

By day two, it's the nights that swelter. I lie awake in my hotel bed, mind-locked: *November 2005. Amman bombings. Three explosions. The Grand Hyatt Hotel. The Days Inn Hotel. The Philadelphia Ballroom of the Radisson. 60 dead.*

On day three, we decide to mix it up a bit, do some sightseeing. Our connect in Amman leaves us with his childhood friend, a taxi driver named Mahmoud. In his thirties, Mahmoud is well groomed and thin. Smokes Marlboro Reds.

Our first stop: Windy Mount Nebo, where God revealed the promised land to prophet Moses.

Many believe God himself buried Moses in that desert mountainside. Standing upon such a holy sight, I decide to spit a rhyme – the only

Negro ever to spit rhymes on Mount Nebo. I hand over the camera and let loose. All the while Mahmoud smiles and claps.

On the way back to the car, we hear the tinny baseline of 50 Cent's "In Da Club": *When I pull out up front, you see the Benz on dubs. When I roll 20 deep, it's 20 knives in the club.* I look at the crew, assuming the song came from one of their cell phones. We're all surprised when the older Arab gentlemen guarding Mount Nebo claims responsibility. When we mine this quirk for humor, Mahmoud jumps in: "We love this music."

By the time we get to the Dead Sea, Mahmoud has played every rap song he owns, including the industry standards: Tupac, 50 Cent, and Eminem. Somehow N'Sync made it into the rotation, which, along with the truth about the resting place of Moses, will remain a mystery.

We stomp the sand to lakeshore, Earth's lowest elevation. Mahmoud points across the Dead Sea to Israel, tells us about his family's displacement from Palestine. Then his face changes. Eyes narrowed to squint in midday sun. Focusing into the distance. *What? What? Did Sharon launch rockets? Was it Al Queda? Bin Laden? The ghost of Idi Amin?* The previous days' paranoia actualize as if on cue.

The Dead Sea is so mineral rich you can float atop the water. Maybe that's why no one on the beach pays mind to the body of an 8-year-old girl, capsized, arms flailing. Mahmoud immediately responds: "Idris! Go! Quickly! That girl! She is drowning!"

I take off into the water like some sort of black Hasslehoff, navigating sharp rocks, head high above the salty current. The closer I get, the harder I pray the girl's just goofing around, but I see her body convulsing.

Nine times saltier than ocean water, a drop from the Dead Sea conjures a burning discomfort. Not even animals survive this lake. And this girl's face is submerged underwater. Dense salt down her throat, up her nose. Her eyes must feel like fire.

Safely back on shore, I expect droves of on-lookers to rush to our aid. But most are detached, as if the event is some shared hallucination between Mahmoud, the girl and myself. The daughter of an indentured Egyptian family of servants and farmers, the girl is of little concern to Jordanian society. We are but three anonymous silhouettes as the blazing sun sets into Israel.

Mahmoud and I talk into the evening, our discussion of class dovetailing into race. The Jordan Rift Valley floods purple, then slate. In the darkness he admits he's always wanted to visit the US. "Sure, sure," his friends tell him, "but make sure to stay away from the blacks."

He explains that in Jordan, black men are typecast as criminals, thugs, gang members. I think back to Mahmoud's thugged out soundtrack en route to the Dead Sea, remember the billboards for Hollywood gangster movies dotting downtown Amman. There is little with which to counter balance.

Then I remember my restless nights in the hotel, bomb strapped Arabs detonating my dreams.

People who look like Mahmoud. People who look like me. The same meglo-media corporations feeding fear across the globe, the glue that binds our shared ignorance.

Perhaps Jordan and the United States aren't so far apart after all.

Our conversation slows to awkward silence. Finally we joke that maybe someone videotaped us on the beach today. Maybe the documentary title would read: *Young Black American and Young Muslim Jordanian Save Life*. "That would be something," he says.

THE IDRIS GOODWIN DOJO FOR THE RHYMING ARTS

The Idris Goodwin Dojo for the Rhyming Arts, where we unlock the secrets of the universe through circular wordplay.

It'll be a storefront. Big glass window at a busy intersection. Adjacent a public park, maybe, a few doors down from 7-11. Eight hundred square feet, office in the back.

Painted in the window: a microphone juxtaposed against red rising sun. Our mantra: "I can take a phrase that's rarely heard, flip it. Now it's the daily word."[6]

At the Idris Goodwin Dojo for the Rhyming Arts, we recognize that letters are symbols, and these symbols represent sound. *All praise to almighty assonance!* Sessions begin with 45 minutes of uninterrupted freestyle. *All praise to allusion!* We explore breath control, vocal dynamics, time. *All praise to the couplet!* Anyone who wants to learn — from six to sixty — we're open seven days a week, twelve hours a day.

We make homes for ourselves within the break beats, beat box, boom box. We spar by example. We love supreme all things. Celebrate those who lock into a groove, ride it into infinity.

Displayed in glass case: white, yellow, green, blue, brown, black, and red microphones. Bait.

At the Idris Goodwin Dojo for the Rhyming Arts, we honor the circles that shape us. Global. Familial. *All praise to the circularity of breath, voice, time!* T-shirts, of course. Perhaps an annual picnic. Mostly we comb the limits of linguistic possibility. *All praise to the*

---

6   A line from Rakim's "Follow the Leader"

subversion of language! Invented slang splayed across mats, on walls. All *praise to bars, measures, verse!*

We infiltrate high and low. Innocuous seeming, deadly, we code switch societies with ease. *All praise to the theft of information!* We break boardrooms, stand on blocks, exhibit. *All praise to relevance!* We spar by example, kill for the confidence to exist fully, without explanation or apology.

There are no record deals here, no endorsements. Instead, we offer praise. Each session is salutation, success. And we don't even have to take off our shoes.

THE GANGSTER RAP QUESTION

I make much of my living preaching the good word of hip-hop. Often I am invited to perform in spaces with a limited view of the culture, so I am asked to engage in talkbacks. To clarify, to expand on that which my performance pieces leave foggy. And I answer a lot of questions. But every now and again, I'm asked the unanswerable.

Consider my varied responses to the question, "Is gangster rap bad?"

I.
Before we take aim, we must first consider our national pastime and the flesh we eat while we watch.

II.
Many times I am told, "I didn't care about rap until I heard NWA." So my question is, if a gangster rapper makes a threat and no one is there to cower, did he really make a sound?

III.
Do you mean "bad" like "good" in that 50's motorcycle way? Bad like James Dean riding along the credit roll?

IV.
Criminal Minds now lecture the Ivy League. Cop Killers now flash a badge between commercials breaks. Ice Cube burnt Hollywood. Once the smoke cleared, he made family movies.

V.
I am watching Snoop Dogg. It's a weekday afternoon. Snoop is stirring brownie batter, bantering thinly veiled weed jokes. Teaching the waspy host and her waspy audience how to rap.

VI.
We must consider what has been forced within the casing.

VII.
And now we invite you to stick your ear to the curb. And if you
listen closely enough you can hear dice collide against spray-painted
brick. And this, this is how you bail out a relative from jail.

Have you ever been so hungry? Has claustrophobia undulated from
your lack of options? Has dying been your best, nagging and frequent
option? Have you felt the surge when reminded that life is fragile?

Now the bullet will graze *your* halo.

This is how to weave slang into a noose. Keep harm at bay from your
body.

VIII.
There is a story. Something about Eazy E attending the 1992
Republican National Convention. A big hiphop no-no. Ice Cube
called him out on record, repeating, "I never had dinner with the
President. I never had dinner with the President."

It's doubtful, of course, that Eazy E actually met Bush, but I have
reoccurring visions.

Eazy entering the Oval Office, white haired, olive skinned manager
Jerry Heller in tow. Bush flanked by Secret Servicemen as he rises
from his leather armchair. Bush asking Eazy to sit, please. A warm
smile slowly forming on his face.

In my imagination, the two reminisce on the old days. Cat and
mouse. FBI letters, CIA files. Feeble attempts at censorship.

Bush asks Eazy to sign a CD for his son, Junior. Eazy asks for tax
advice. Bush asks for tips on dealing drugs. Bush asks if the group
will ever get back together. Eazy asks if the military will ever get out
of Iraq.

I imagine Bush touring Eazy through the Situation Room, showing
off his artillery collection. Eazy recognizing many of the high-

powered rifles. Bush revealing weapons Eazy's only dreamt of.

White haired, olive skinned manager Jerry Heller suggesting that
Eazy should work in government. Eazy suggesting that Bush become
his new manager. Bush laughing at them both.

IX.
We must consider the blood harvest that gets us through the winter.

X.
Who runs Ivy League secret societies? Who produces NBC? Who
makes Girls Gone Wild? Who lobbies?

Who operates the satellites, the milk and produce, that give you
cancer? Who buys real estate on the moon? Who owns patents on
plants and bone marrow? Who defines the dictionary? Who forced
that foreign language into my mouth? And who has the biggest body
count? Tell me, who has got the biggest body count?

XI.
The real threat drifts silent. Hides where few turn to look. And
rappers, they talk too much. Kids like the sound of their *ratta tata tat*
flow. Similar to the sounds of war they've long grown accustomed to,
ever since the first toy soldier was thrust into their tiny hands.

A FOUND ESSAY

This is an essay about the word Nigger.

SEVEN REMIXES OF THE PHONOGRAM

"One of the hardest instruments we have tried to record is the organ, and the easiest is the English concertina. Negros take better than white singers because their voices have a certain sharpness or harshness about them that a white singer has not. A barking dog, squalling cat, neighing horse and in fact, almost any beast or birds voice is excellent for the good repetition on a record."
—The Phonogram, 1891[7]

Remix #1
One of the noises we've tried to record is Negro English.

Remix #2
It's easiest to record a Negro with a harsh record.

Remix #3
A barking Negro is a hard organ.

Remix #4
Certain white English singers have tried to record their Negro voices.

Remix #5
White and Negro. A record of harsh, sharp barking in repetition.

Remix #6
Try the white horse, Bird!

Remix #7
A good voice is birds and white squalls. An excellent voice has harshness.

---

7   The Phonogram was the first industry trade newspaper of the burgeoning recording industry.

WHISTLING

North Americans squeezed themselves under state fair tents to hear a faint duplicated sound. Though the simple songs were crushed beneath yards of crackling distortion, the audience was amazed. Still, Edison and company knew the phonograph could be better. They just needed a powerful enough voice singing the right words. Enter George W Johnson, an ex slave, a street performer of the popular minstrel songs of the mid 1800's. He was an exceptional mimic of sound, a skill he honed emulating the violin played on the Virginia plantation by Master Johnson's son.

It was his impeccable laugh. *The Laughing Coon* had been sung by a million cork faced white guys but George's take was infectious. His clarity on phonograph was unparalleled. His version became a fast hit, as was his follow up *The Whistling Song*. They called him "Dandy Darkey."

George's vocal prowess lined Edison's pockets while he only took home pennies. He would sing the same two songs, thousands of takes swallowed. Millions of each carefully crafted laugh and whistle over and over and over and over and over again. George became one of the most successful recording stars, living as high as someone of his background could in that time. He kept laughing until eventually alcoholism and scandal, slowed his rotation.

But now, after more than a century he's performing at this year's music awards. Straight off the cobblestone, no one was more street than him. They're gonna put him on a rotating stage in his vest, ruffled cuffs, even a white wig — they want him to blow the dust off his two hits. The world awaits but is unaware that George kept his face to the glass. He's gonna sing his two standards but at the end his cheeks wont ascend to laugh. His lips wont purse to whistle. George has a plan reworked for over a century The phonograph was ambivalent to his origin, his destination. It consumed his endless takes of endless laughter and infinite whistle and infinite, his endless darkness. For pennies. He's going to demand his royalties.

He's gonna end it on air live at the music awards, give us a glimpse of the future. Tell us something beautiful . He's gonna kill it dead for ever. Over and over and over and over and over again. He will change everything.

ELECTION YEAR

Is America ready for the very first organic, non-hydrogenated, soy, partially sun-dried, distilled, natural spring alloy? Alternative, green, poly-cultural, poly-amorous? The first multi-tri-bimono-minded? The first vegan-friendly, pro-life, all choice, all satellite, 24-hour digital?

Is America ready to finally run this nation like an assembly line? To push its gears, cheese its wheel, calm its cattle, whistle its Dixie, ladle its soup?

Is it ready to wash its hands before returning to work? To reinvent the dime? Balance a quarter on its nose while riding a unicycle?

Is it full throttle, heavy metal enough to go the distance? To be woven onto the front of a jean jacket? To be shot out of a cannon, stuffed into a trunk? To be made over in just 12 hours? To be married on an exotic island to a… pomegranate!

Is America strong enough, mature enough? Has it healed? Has it lived in a grass hut?

Been in the Peace Corps? Denounced its upbringing and grown a longer beard? Has it sang loudly enough for the judges? Has it completed all of the physical requirements? Can it walk the runway? Can it lose the weight?

Is it ready for the first self-propelled, self-medicated, self-aware, self-loathing?

Can it handle the impact of a full-fledged wavering moderate neutralist with right wing tendencies and a sympathy for 1960's beach films?

Is America ready?

Oh, but we've uncovered blemishes. Dental records. Bounced checks. Red headed step kids. We've opened official transcripts. Re-taped those shredded memos. Screened home movies, dug up the bones, dusted the skeletons for prints!

And it's all become clear. The puzzle pieces fit and, quite frankly, this is unlike anything America has seen in its lifetime.

But isn't it's long overdue? Shouldn't we bring out the cavalcade of oddities and anomalies?! The things that make us crinkle and scowl, that make smoke steam from our ears, that bring back sore memories like when we kissed our cousin on the mouth.

Accidentally.

According to our online poll, America couldn't be more ready!

a U.F.O sighting, a Miley-Cyrus, a fried bucket of chicken, a PT Barnum and Bailey circus.

Would elect a donut if it promised cheaper gas, could pop lock, slash, burn, cut, run, turn the other cheek, bite off the nose and Disco ball non-stop!

PRE, POST AND CURRENTLY RACIAL AMERICA

I didn't ask to get involved.

Back in 2008 when Obama accepted his presidential nomination the strangest thing happened. Middle-aged white people began stopping me in the street, at the grocery store, while hiking, to engage in random racial dialogue.

I should've been encouraged by these open exchanges. When I was coming up, the only people interested in public conversations about race were fellow victims of racism. Otherwise it was pure snowy silence. That was the hip multicultural maxim, anyway. I-don't-see-color, except of course for that whole OJ thing.

So it was jarring when the goofy eyes, knowing nods from strangers started up. They'd awkwardly shift from "Nice weather we're having" to rambling trips down memory lane: the 60's, when Peace and Harmony interlocked hands in a grand gesture of solidarity, when Motown arched its soulful cords to bridge racial borders and so on and so on.

It all took a turn when I worked at an outdoor newsstand in downtown Santa Fe, New Mexico, however.

Santa Fe is the sort of place where every store, restaurant, and avenue has a Spanish or American Indian name, yet all of the native New Mexicans are nowhere in sight. So it should come as no surprise that while Santa Fe has an abundance of sunlight and turquoise jewelry, it is desperately lacking in the 30ish-year-old black guy department. You get what I'm saying.

So there I was, on a busy Santa Fe street in the central Plaza, tourists bustling about, shopping bags weighed down with hand chiseled brown figurines. I'm parked on a folding chair, my big head eclipsing rows and rows of glossy magazines. Magazines featuring, you guessed it, everyone's favorite brown politician on the cover. I was an easy target.

The day after Obama won the primary, someone yelled from across the street — maybe 20 feet away — "I bet *you're* happy!" Considering the logic, this woman should have been punch drunk when McCain won his respective primary. After all, he is old, white *and* rich. Of course, I never said that. I am no agitator.

I didn't even respond to the lady who bought a bottle of water, then shook her head conspiratorially, whispering, "Can you believe he picked Biden? Always gotta shoulder up with the white man, right?"

As Obama fervor grew, my individuality seemed to shrink, until I was just another brown figurine hocked on a Santa Fe sidewalk.

I was anxious for the whole democracy thing to hurry up, get decided already. Then maybe the tokenism would stop and interracial relations could resort back to old habits. What was so bad about tiptoeing around the race maypole, anyway?

The truth was that it was hard enough for me to deal with my own day-to-day trials without acting as the sounding board for white wish fulfillment, without providing misplaced redemption for an entire generation of aging leftists. This will all be over soon, I told myself.

But then he won. And it dawned on me: I've got four more years of this. Maybe eight.

Suddenly, inexplicably, my great great great grandfather appeared beside me on my maroon leather couch. Obama's speech still hanging in the air, the ghost of my grandfather to my right, and me, stunned frozen in between.

Of course, I immediately apologized for not keeping in better touch. "You can shove that apology," he said, a sort of raspy bark. His eyes narrowed. "Don't you know that it used to be illegal for black people to vote? That it used to be illegal for black people *to be people?*"

He continued on and on like the ghosts of our great great great grandfathers tend to do, enumerating all of the privileges I enjoy as a child of the 21st century. "The last thing you should concern yourself with," he said, "are white people who openly praise a black man. Are they vying to lynch him? No. Are they betting on him to win the Superbowl? No. Just let them be, boy."

And with that, he was gone. So were my petty annoyances. For the first time in months, I experienced peace with my role. In fact, from then on, I welcomed tourist testimonials and opinions. The last thing I wanted to do is come off as rude.

I no longer sell newspapers in Santa Fe and gone are the abrupt professions of racial solidarity. Immediately following the election, pundits posed the question: "Now that this black guy is president, hasn't America moved past this whole race thing?"[8] Now its a post racial America in which congratulations are given for sitting through all five seasons of *The Wire*. "Diversity" is "celebrated" during the months designated for such activity. We swing with equal velocity at our *politician du jour* for unfulfilling our projected promises. We ignore the tangled fabric and dance circles around the maypole.

---

8   I am paraphrasing

10 UP: REFLECTIONS ON THE FIRST DECADE OF OUR NEW MILLENNIUM

We had zeroes in our eyes, fearful of a cybernetic revolt. And then: zilch. Sun up, sun down, 2000 revolved in proper rotation. The next day, we returned to our plates of venture capital. Fat on Tarantino, all bling and diamond breath.

Fall forward to November's Tuesday, when the unlikeliest name flashed the screen. The century's first Executive crime-spree. And we, limp bystanders, hit the bar. Rounds and shots, shots and rounds. We all got loaded.

After that: silence. A quiet eerie, a corn choked prairie. And then, one morning, our creation myth erupted. A plot point jammed, flag-like, into billowing cement. Before. And after.

What followed was Evil and Freedom, twins howling a hollow howl. The red blare of it rattling us out of our bong haze, down the meth pipe. What followed were more Adventures in Arabia.

Somebody shot Dionysus! His chest broke and released: silhouettes hanging from helicopter blades, HELP lettered in blood, soaked limbs, drowning crescent. All of it live on the 10 o'clock news.

"Too little too late."

Followed by rolled sleeves, a wink and utterance repeated,

"Mourn?"
"Laugh again?"
"Forget?"

Lands holy desecrated, ancient wounds punctured. We caught Saddam in a hole on a farm and on Eid he was hanged. The site bounced from pole to pole, but the twins, they still howled, the red blare blared.

> Cue the police states.
> Cue the women, the children.

This, our global village, our backyard, where police shoot men unarmed. The hush-hush of power familiar. Justice kidnapped like young women in desert slums, young women whose bodies fade forgotten, narrow bones windswept by the shushing lips of patriarchy.

Torture photos arrived on schedule. Propositions debated, overturned.

> Cue the outrage.

Still the crescent sinks. Still the smoke — at our feet, above our heads — pollutes our dreams blind. Still the masses wander broken, pondering Evil, Freedom.

It has been rugged. We wear it in our shoulders, this tension. The young and old, something in us has shattered.

Hope, we don't need it. On this precipice what we need is justice.

BLACK SANTA

From the outside: identical. Cookie cut three-level Midwestern houses. And Greg, he was average, too. Michigan bred, suburban raised. Frame of reference cable provided.

It was jarring, I suppose, Greg's trip down to the basement, down the stairs to leather couch, oversized TV and video games. First, we had to shortcut through the kitchen. Deep earth tones, the lingering vinegar of last night's greens. Then the living room. Walls of wide-eyed wooden masks, coffee table glossy with black celebrities. And finally, the foyer. Black angels crowning the Christmas tree. Beyond that, Santa Claus.

"You have a black Santa?" he blurted, pure sarcastic delight. I didn't get the joke. "Yeah, sure," I said, forced smile. If we had a female Santa, perhaps that'd be something of note. If our Santa was a ball of yarn, or even a cyborg, then maybe I'd see his point. Still, he persisted, my confusion egging his astonishment. "Don't you think that's kind of extreme? Black Santa!" It certainly made for an awkward afternoon of video gaming.

Now, I had been a guest in countless neighborhood homes, all well stocked with Norman Rockwell and Better Homes and Gardens. Never was I dazed by the over-representation of white skin. And yet, somehow, our deviation of standard décor had morphed into defiance, hostility. I imagined my parents — a corporate engineer, a city planner — as fist pumping Panthers, and laughed.

Looking back, it's true our Santa was political. But I didn't know that then. There was Normal Santa, White Guy Santa. I saw him everywhere. But the guy in red who came knocking on our door, the one who smelled like the grown up's eggnog, he was black like my parents. Black like my pastor. Like Jesus.

On the sanctuary walls of eastside Detroit's New Calvary Baptist, the church where I spent over 900 Sundays as a kid, there are two large paintings of Jesus. In each portrait, God's son sports a nicely glowing natural. Once a predominately white Lutheran church, New Calvary transitioned into all black Baptist when it applied brown paint to Jesus' pale features.

The back and forth over my Jesus' skin tone seems mote in comparison to larger debates. Like, say, Jesus' take on Roe v. Wade. Or which professional quarterback he'll support this season. When it comes to Santa Claus, though, we may as well be discussing Barbie doll. Santa's nothing more than a red-ribboned advertising campaign, a parent's last defense in the war with their kids. Not to mention, he's supplied us with black Barbies since the 1960's.

I wonder if other ethnicities employ the services of a Secret Santa, the subversive sort that mirrors their own physical attributes. Is there an Indian Santa? A Chinese Santa?

My future child will be bi-racial. Black and Chicano. And we will no doubt fold under the weight of American tradition by entangling ourselves in the Santa Claus ballyhoo. Why should our bi racial daughter be denied? But will we buy two separate Santa figurines? Or make our own? Put some gators and a red hat on a Dora The Explorer doll? Maybe we'll just go with female Santa and call it a day.

SOL FOOD

The scattered forgotten collected, concocted. Blood and heart, hooves and knees, jowls and ears and skin and innards. Yes, the innards. Yards and yards and yards. Boiled 'til they swell sweet over flame. Then onions, celery, carrots, cayenne.

The stomach's howl fades to whimper.

Or else bottom feeders. All that dirt infused funk. Robust, bursting like garlic cloves spanked by the wooden spoon. Peppered, fused, snug in cornhusk cradle, cheesecloth, dough, rock salt.

Carried across tundra, barren lands that stretch from eye to infinity. Carried on the backs of pack animals by tribes you didn't know you belonged to. Each bites spills stories traded over continents just like spices and human beings.

Put your ear to the pan. Hear that symphony of flour and salt and egg wash rubbed between tendons. All that wonderful sizzle splatters across Sunday tablecloths. Lace made transparent, white shirts ruined, neckties smeared.

We are not just Wonderbread and mayonnaise!

We are gumbo, blistering jambalaya, arroz con pollo, su frito, pallella, shrimp and grits, carne adobada, sopapillas.

We are not just ketchup and jelly beans!

We are chicharrones, pork rinds, chutney, cha cha, salsa and guacamole, udon noodles slurped from hot pots, chicken feet sticking out the broth like birthday candles.

We are the crock pot, the wok. We are hot curry, smooth ground chickpeas, lemon and parsley. We are shellfish snatched from murky water, sautéed, coaxed open to sing.

We are not just a drive through window. We are a nation of soul food, and we taste *damn* good.

SHOW AND PROVE

Third shift: 11:30 pm to 7:30 am. If you fall asleep, you're fired.

The Chrysler Proving Grounds in Chelsea, Michigan covers 3,850 acres of rural Michigan prairie. Round the clock driving on simulated terrains, high-speed tracks verifying vehicles' predetermined limits. If an animal wanders in your wake, keep going. Raccoons mostly. The occasional possum, deer. Don't swerve. Don't stop the system. You don't never stop the line.

Some nights, there are new sleek concept cars. UK models with the steering wheel on the right. Other nights, rusted shells, no radio. Manual transmission. Shift one to five, than shift back down. Repeat. How much did the vehicle rattle? Rate the rattle. 1 means a lot, 5 means not enough.

All eyes are on the recent hire: the boss' kid. Jobs are scarce in Chelsea. There's a long line of guys who can stay up with the best of 'em.

Use ice-cold water. Use coffee. Crank the music up loud. Use books on tape, mysteries and pulp novels. The growing suspense, accentuated by Joe Mantegna's masterful recitation, use that to stay awake.

Take pills to stay awake at night. Take pills to sleep in the day. How effective are the pills? Rate the pills. 1 means a lot, 5 means not enough.

When your eyelids became too heavy, when the smooth sound of asphalt is replaced with tearing grass and mud thump, slam on the breaks. Take deep breaths. But don't stop the line.

Develop a new technique. Use freestyling to keep your brain and body active. Conduct concerts, pretend to be a line-up of imagined acts: backpacking metaphysical weed head; diamond soaked nightclub connoisseur; esoteric space man avant-guardian; hillbilly moonshiner; defiant mime; roving psychopath; fast food chain mascot; and so on.

Manipulate your voice. Vary your cadence. Shift one to five, than shift back down. Repeat. Use a tape recorder. Document elaborate rap operas.

Meld mystery and rap, use that to stay awake. Sample the reoccurring plot devices of Ed Mcbain and Walter Mosely. A record label CEO turns up dead; uncover who-done-it.[9]

You, alone in the woods. Talking to yourself. Listening to yourself. Man; son; rapper; writer. How effective are you? Rate yourself. 1 means a lot, 5 means not enough.

---

9   It was the DJ.

A POOR PROFESSION

"Mainstream rap is a scam. It makes people believe you can get rich from rapping. Rap is one of the poorest art forms on the planet Earth."
— *KRS ONE*

Das Efx aside, rappers have never lived underground. We walk among you as bank tellers, teachers, electricians. Stay at home moms and stay at home dads. Some of our most talented work for UPS others for pubs. We pour you that perfect Guinness from behind the bar, wishing on foamy four-leaf clovers for another late night gig, another payout.

But beer-soaked wads of cash never did stretch far. At least not for Russ, an MC who works days at Kinkos. Unlimited free flyers for all the shows he books. Promotes. Headlines.

Maria, she's an MC who works double shift at Radio Shack. 10% discounts on spool after spool of blank CDs.

Dante, he's on your couch right now. Spends more than half the year in a van, eager for any electrical outlet that will have him. He'll settle a few months to work hardhat construction, than do it all over again.

Mellee Mel and Grandmaster Caz, they never had a 401K. Never had a writing retreat at Martha's Vineyard. They only had their name, broke but not broken.

Rappers, we're of bunch of big mouths wielding all manner of speech, a worldwide community on a quest for nothing, for everything. For infinity: that next couplet, and the one after that. We are the postmodern poet laureates of the Digital Age, desperate for recognition from a society blind enough to believe that stars fall from the sky.

Yolanda, her big rap advance was conquering her speech impediment. And Arianna, her rap payoff was learning English after emigrating to the U.S. from Israel. The best rappers in the West Bank and in Gaza, they can't connect because of international human rights violations. Yet they bend borders with grammar, composing new laws in cipher.

Enough of romance. We are a naïve, shortsighted lot, fulfilled by audiences explosive, hearts hungry, thumping in pace to a well-timed letter. Glut on gas money and merch moved. Then, when the show dies and it's quiet again, we struggle to drown out your demands. "Come down from the ledge," you say. "Make sense. Give up the dream."

But we can't stop rocking this dream because it's a path, not a dream at all but a conduit to decipher humanity's coded language. We may quit Kinkos or Radio Shack, but there's no retiring this road.

LORD FINESSE VS. PERCEE P: A PLAY-BY-PLAY

The screen is fuzzy but the sound is good. A break beat snaps in the background, music thumping the Bronx playground alert. In the foreground, urbanites crowd street side, inquisitively eyeballing the camera.

It's 1989 and it's summer – you can see it – everyone's outside, limbs bared. The little guy in the big fisherman's hat introduces himself into the tiny microphone. "Yo, I be the Grand Imperial Lord Finesse from the Bronx projects," he says.

A dark skinned brother in gold chain lights up. On spot, he becomes the commentator of upcoming events.

"Hello, my name is Tony Webb and I'm like, a scholar," he says. "Today the most main event, aqui, is my man Lord Finesse from Uptown against – the who? – the Chief Wizard Inspector Percee P."

A slim, lanky brother in a red button down shirt makes his way through the small crowd.

"Now, Percee P, what do you have say about this event tonight?" the host asks.

Soft-spoken, Percee P's voice is too low, too far from the microphone, to make out.

"Now, Lord Finesse, what do you have to say?"

"I aint trying to take no loss."

"As you can see," the host says, "both individuals are ready for a win. So we will now see what happens." He pauses, smiles big. Then, when he assumes the camera is off, his smile drops. "Did you stop it?" he asks the cameraman.

The screen goes fuzzy, then we slam straight into the next shot: back street side, crowd anxious for battle. Our host is back on the job. "Round one of the main event," he says.

Someone yells, "Ding, ding."

We hear the click of a tape deck. A beat starts to play, but it's too slow, not at all right. A few moments later, another click; the iconic "Funky Drummer" blasts the speakers. Its energetic tempo and stripped down texture make it the perfect outdoor battle beat. A summer evening showdown.

Lord Finesse's head hangs low as he searches for his footing inside the beat. When he finally looks up, he says, surprised, "Oh, I gotta go first? " Most battlers would rather go second. "Fuck it," he says. But just as he is about to begin, Percee P steps into the frame and launches into verse.

I rap with knowledge/ lines compiled in a complex style/ Convey 'em/ intricately say 'em, slay 'em and exile/Wild rap competitors get ready for my metaphoric phrase

His flow is nimble, words flipping, dancing within the break. He conducts his verbal symphony of expensive scientific terms and neighborhood slang with arms that sway and slice the air. Off–camera, we hear someone from Percee P's crew backing him up, emphasizing certain lines for greater impact.

Rap fans remember me for my lyrical chemistry/ Brains might explode, knowledge overloads my memory bank/ Clever whoever has it and don't pass it/ I'll burn 'em like boric or hydrochloric acid

His verse is futuristic. Even now, twenty years later, few contemporary rappers can pull off this style convincingly. Despite his innovative artistry, the crowd has yet to explode. They're engaged, sure — you'd have to be dead not to be — but they have yet to hit the floor in reaction to a knock out line. But Percee is determined to crush his competitor early on, you can see it in his face. The momentum builds and builds and builds. An unstoppable train.

If you diss me or piss me off/ I'm a stomp you quick/ Strictly poetical/ dope notes/ I wrote from my throat/Quoted in papers/ folks catchin the vapors is a result/ Laugh at ya like a psycho, might go after ya worse than the Valentine or Chainsaw Massacre

Lord Finesse has his work cut out for him. Such a lengthy and highly technical first verse is tough to follow. By now, the crowd has grown larger. Two teenage girls in doorknocker earrings and a man cradling his baby daughter nod their heads to the beat as Lord Finesse jumpstarts. His style is not nearly as dexterous as Percee P's. It's slower, easier to follow, and laced with humor.

Finesse, now I'm smooth sensational educational, here to awaken you/ On top of you, rocking you, here to get popular/ Me fall off? Picture that with binoculars

He drops the first major pop culture reference of the battle: MacGyver. Thumbs pop up one after another in the crowd.

Equipped for an emergency, don't try burning me/ I get poonany, plus keep the currency

Some raunchy language to wake the crowd. The teenage girls buckle in response, study one another's faces, then flash a thumbs up in the camera.

Finesse's verse was significantly shorter and not nearly as complex as his opponent's, but Finesse has proven that he's not intimidated in the least by Percee P's flashy wordplay. It's his persona, that infectious confidence, that he relies on instead.

The camera cuts to our host, Tony Webb, who returns to announce round two.

Percee P comes out of the corner more ferocious than ever.

No one survives/ so why make a sequel

In the crowd, his hype man has taken on a bigger role, now echoing entire phrases. Picking up the rhyme when Percee P drops it. The whole thing is acrobatic, mesmerizing.

Every week I'm like lottery / rap is a part of me/ words flow but don't show like blood in the artery/ Ladies of the 80's/ treat me just like a star/ "When he show up"/ they throw up they panties and bras.

The verse builds and builds to electric peak, then slowly, inexplicably, starts to simmer. Percee keeps flowing, of course, but something's happened, changed, the lines don't spark with the same confidence. It's as if Percee P's performance shorted, then dimmed ever so slightly.

It's grown darker outside. The teenage girls and the dad with baby have been replaced with sorted neighborhood guys. Lord Finesse feeds off of this new masculine energy. His verse is rife with his multisyllabic assonance, similes, metaphors, and pop culture references.

The crowd smiles at lines like:

My pockets stay fat like a goose down

Putting rhymes in shape like Jack Lalaine

Get schooled and read like a textbook

The funkiest MC out since Shakespeare

The "Funky Drummer" beat blends with the jingle of a Mister Softee truck that's inching up the block. It's the same melody made iconic in Eddie Murphy's ice cream bit from Delirious.

The camera cuts again. Now, the block is covered by nightfall. Our host returns. "Round 3," he says.

Percee P doesn't miss a beat.

Forget the bubble gum pop/ I'm bout to drop science on ya'll

And off he goes. But maybe 30 seconds into his assault, the lights go out again. He rocks silently to the beat, searching for the next line. Minute after minute after minute. This is the battle rapper's worse nightmare, especially during Round 3. Somewhere in the crowd, Percee P's hype man shouts out some lines, hoping to re-ignite the battle.

"Come on," Lord Finesse protests. "You can't have your man helping you remember, now!" Sympathetic, the crowd tries to encourage Percee P. "Do you man! Come on!" Finally, after what to him must have felt like two lifetimes, Percee's back on his flow, but the mistake drifts in night air. Lord Finesse smiles, knows the advantage has swayed his way.

The crowd is thick now. Their attention locked on Lord Finesse. He surges with re-doubled energy, as though he's ciphered Percee P's confidence straight out of him.

I'm fresher/ aint no half stepper/ And I'll bet cha/ mess with me/ and you'll leave in a stretcher/ Nasty/fancy/ rap vigilante/ Get funky/ on the mic cuz it come in handy/ You can't stop this/ Mission accomplished/I burn that ass and I'll leave you unconscious/ Mystical/ magical/ I'm straight waxin you/ Tell me now, am I little too fast for you?

Ooooooohhhhhhhs bubble from the crowd.

Finesse is on fire. His arms illustrate the lyrical dance. Suddenly, he stops. "I'm a leave it like that. I aint even gotta say no more," he says. The crowd concurs.

Cut. The host says, "And now, the final chapter."

Percee P and his hype man are back at it, but the performance is tired. Robotic. Phoned in. He spun his wheels out too early. Percee tries to cut through the obnoxious, looping Mr. Softee jingle, cut through the lingering memory of his slip-up, but to no avail. He is doomed, the rap version of Ali/ Foreman. Percee P has just flat out run out of spark, while Lord Finesse pulled a hip-hop rope a dope.

In his final round, Finesse opts to go sans beat. His clever turns of phrase, his surprising similes stand out, his rhyme pattern sharper than ever. Percee P's dexterity is no match for Lord Finesse's personality.

The final verse. You can feel the crowd hungry for that T.K.O. They want Percee P sent home, licking his wounds.

If rap was money/ you'd be labled as a food stamp

Finesse's right cross dazes Percee, opens the crowd. Then he goes in for the kill.

When I leave, you be askin' where the trouble went/ but don't say shit until your ass get a double mint

The crowd explodes, the battle decided. Lord Fineesse swaggers off into the evening long before Percee P's reputation ever hits the ground.

BREAK BEAT POETRY

When Bronx DJs performed for neighborhood block parties in the early 70s, they discovered how to extend the instrumental "break down" section of a record. When looped, these free-flowing break downs – dubbed break beats – served as the audio stage on which dancers and MCs "got loose" or "styled."[10]

Birthed from the intersection of Afro Latin, Latin jazz, be bop jazz, hard bop, hard rock, rock and roll, rhythm and blues, blue-eyed soul and German computer music, break beats are true poly-cultural relics. All electronic music, from rap to house to techno, drum and bass, utilize the cyclical flow of a break beat.

Break beat music ignited listeners' desire for self-expression, including many writers of the hip-hop generation. Their "God selves were let loose"[11] by the break beat, rousing writers to fracture tradition and sample surprising new structures. Break beat poets play with assonance and repetition, but they also explore possibilities of meter, blending familiar rhythms, melodies, and cadences with the unexpected.

It is an attempt to make music with words. As such, the writing requires careful consideration. In the same manner that a classical composer balances each note, a break beat poet must consider his or her words with precision. A successful break beat poem can (and should) be recorded and published so that the public may fully experience this synthesis of the visual and the aural. It goes without saying that break beat poems are created with the intention to be performed aloud for an audience. They are to be felt, to be "heard

---

10   These were local terms before break dancing or rapping, when individuals
      expressed themselves in response to the DJ's break beats.

11   Refers to a popular quote by hip-hop pioneer Afrika Bambatta: "When I heard
      the break beat, I let my God self get loose."

with the hips."[12]

Break beat poetry attempts to generate a physical response in the bodies of listeners before their brains censor movement. A successful break beat poem will bob heads, tap feet, jump fingers, launch chills, fling words into mouths. It is entirely physical. The poet must feel the urgency of the piece throughout his or her body. The break beat poem can only be experienced if its creator shows the listeners how.

In instances where a break beat poet works with a musical accompaniment, he or she must pay homage to the music as its own form of poetry. The break beat poet's approach, then, should allow for the music to lead, to inspire the writing. Break beat poets often freestyle, but more importantly, they write songs.

It should be noted that break beat poetry is not in defiance of, or in conflict with, any other strain of writing or performance. Instead, it embraces multiple genres, much as early DJ artistry blended funk, soul, and rock. Everything is fair game, as long as it emanates from the raw, un-tampered music of the soul, that patchwork of multiple allegiances, contradictory opinions, and bittersweet experiences.

Most importantly, break beat poets are not afraid. They write with purpose: to celebrate humanity, even when demanding justice. Break Beat Poetry speaks to the concerns, dreams, and hungers of actual living, breathing communities of individuals. Break Beat Poems are honest. Break Beat Poems celebrate.

---

12   Refers to a line by poet Denis Kim: "Listen to this poem with your hips."

SPEECH, SPEECH!

In 2008, I was honored to receive Young Chicago Authors' Wallace Douglas Award for Excellence in Teaching Creative Writing.[13] The following is a speech I gave at the graduation ceremony.

It was my mother's mother who said, "Pat, that boy, he gon' be somebody's preacher." To which I responded with the usual humoring of my grandparents. (Maybe you're great to your grandparents. Maybe you visit them weekly, buy them VHS tapes, listen to their stories about the old country when all they ate were potatoes and lice. Well, not me. I was teenaged and brilliant.) No, I was an Aspiring Artist, intent on mastering the craft of cinema. Stars burned into my eyes. I was going to write, I was going to direct, I was going to score my own gold plated, boxed set, collector's edition DVD action thrillers.

Naturally, upon high school graduation I enrolled in Chicago's Columbia College to train in the deadly Film Arts. I was the kind of ass-kissing movie dork that film school professors loved, Judo throwing classmates who dared to say that Hitchcock was overrated, fore-knuckle fisting others who complained that Spike Lee was a misogynistic hack.

Like I said, maybe you call your grandparents every night and sing them lullabies. Whatever, that's not what this is about.

After graduating film school with Honors (Honors Jenkins, a classmate of mine), I set out to actualize on my skills, to become a valuable member of filmmaking high society. But I didn't want to uproot, certainly not to New York City or Hollywood. Instead, I stayed put in America's Slaughterhouse, good old Chicago.

---

13 For more information about Young Chicago Authors or the YCA Saturday Writing Program, visit www.youngchicagoauthors.org.

After some weeks of pavement-hitting, job-hunting agony, I landed
a gig in the industry as a page for the Jenny Jones Show. Mostly I
worked the green rooms, made sure guests didn't kill one another
until the cameras were rolling. An overgrown babysitter, I supervised
a whole slew of Barnum and Bailey oddities: spiky-haired, badass
teens and reunited high school sweethearts and critically obese twin
sisters. One time, I babysat all of the cash money millionaires. Juvie,
Birdman, Lil' Wayne. Nothing significant to say about that, though.
They were actually pretty polite, ordinary guys.

Day after day, I would sit in the green room, maybe next to a
Ginuwine impersonator rehearsing his upcoming set, maybe not. I'd
sit there thinking that maybe this isn't exactly the path I'd intended.
Maybe, just maybe, I need to take some drastic action.

So I did what most terrified young artists do. I went back to school.

Against the advice of my film school mentors, I enrolled in The
School of the Art Institute of Chicago's MFA Writing Program.
"They're all experimental over there," a former professor said, but
I didn't care. At Columbia College, I was schooled in Birth of a
Nation and traditional three-act screenplays. I learned how to cut
film the old-fashioned way with razor blades and clear tape, how to
write a properly formatted screenplay, how to direct actors to convey
emotion. I learned how to execute a script like the big boys, how to
make art the way it's been done for decades.

What they didn't teach me was how to explore, how to improvise,
how to fail. It was true, The School of The Art Institute was wildly
experimental, and I liked it. It was unfettered craziness. During
our first meeting together, my graduate advisor said, "I like your
screenplay. It feels like stageplay. Why don't you write a play and
I'll put it up in my theater festival." Then he got up from his chair,
grabbed his coat, and walked out of the room.

Did I know anything about theater? Nope. But why the hell not
take him up on his offer? (I learned why the hell not some three

productions later, but that's another story.) Nevertheless, I was branching out, exploring new territory. My first play starred two of my college buddies. Produced in a small café/theater, the play was rife with limitations, but I savored the experience. I was a quick study, learning from my numerous mistakes, stomaching bad reviews, celebrating the small victories. Film became less and less my sole mode of expression. I had evolved into a playwright.

Now, I'm not here today to talk about how we became writers. I'm here to talk about how to nurture our adventurous spirit, how to be explorers of life. Curious and persistent, passionate and foolish.

Let's take a detour, talk jazz for a second.

It wasn't until I stood in front of a room of teenagers at Harlan Academy, way down there past where the redline stops, that I really learned what jazz music was all about. You have this much space from here to here. From there to there. To travel that short distance, you could go in a straight line. It'll certainly get you to your destination most quickly, but there's no surprise. The students at Harlan Academy were not interested in straight lines. Working that classroom was like playing in a jazz band. I had to listen, had to respond, harmonize, lay back, all in attempt to create and sustain a particular vibe. When it's time to solo, you better not hesitate, or it's all over. In those Chicago public school classrooms with their mind-numbing florescent lights and bland, prison colored walls, it can be a real challenge to play good music.

What makes this writing community so special is not that you are kooky and creative and want to be writers so that you can ya-da-ya-da to society and the art world. No, what makes this community so special is the space itself. Not the physical space, but the creative, open, free space to jam. The communal understanding that each and every Saturday, we will conduct a symphony of professional experience and fresh new perspectives, underscored by insecurity and playfulness.

Sure, we are the instructors and you the scholars, but the truth of the matter is, we're just riffing together.

We're having an informal jam session, letting our chaos and poetry coalesce into something that can't be simulated in the traditional classroom. Writing communities like this one push us to trust in our collective musical abilities in a way that few schools would allow. You've proven yourselves explorers of life by stepping foot outside of your familiar neighborhoods in search of knowledge.

My route took the form of colleges and institutes. But maybe you'll choose a different path. Maybe you want to learn how to get your cobble on, move to Ireland, become an apprentice. Maybe you want to push an Italian Ice cart or road manage Levert. Maybe you want to drive a rig, hustle money on the side arm wrestling at trucker bars. Not all of you will become professional writers, and that's a good thing. Whatever you choose — and you can choose many options simultaneously — don't worry if it's lucrative. When people ask, "How will you make money as an asparagus farmer?" you respond, "Hand over fist, that's how!" Because being a grownup doesn't mean that you have to wear a suit and tie everyday and creative writing — creative living — can't be taught. It can only be encouraged, nurtured, applauded.

Best of luck to all of you. You've come to the end of phase one, and now you initiate into a wider world of possibilities. Don't be afraid to ask for help. And I don't mean like helping you move out of your apartment. I mean, ask for the things that scare you, the things that make you nervous. The things you feel you don't deserve.

Seriously, though, don't ask me to help you move. Everything else is fair game.

Don't be afraid. You're creative, which means you know how to improvise. How to take a phrase and flip it, turn it into a surprise. Be in the band, always. Keep that song going. And when it's time to play your solo, blare it with all the honesty and flair that you can muster.

I wish you the best, the worst, the wild, the downright disgusting, and all of the unforgettable, mindaltering rest.

FALLIN' OFF

In 1992, rap legend KRS ONE (considered by hip-hop fans as "The Teacher"), together with an unidentified entourage, stormed the stage of pop sensation PM Dawn.

My name is Attrell, but they call me Prince Be. I'm a vocalist, a poet. Not a rapper. My brother DJ Minutemix and I make up the group PM Dawn. We're just a couple of brothers from Jersey. Our stepfather — he's a musician, too — played with Kool and the Gang.

You might've heard our brand of hip-hop inspired easy listening, maybe on your drive home from work. We sample a lot of British soft rock. Our single "Set Adrift On Memory's Bliss" might remind you of Spandau Ballet's "True." At least that's what we'd hoped.

We're a far cry from the tough guy. I guess you could say we've crossed sonic borders. Those hardcore hip-hop heads call us soft. Say we're not real. Question our sexuality. But me, I think that every guy has something feminine in us, and vise versa. That's just the way it is. I wonder if rock bands go through such hazing. I imagine they can select their volume without threat.

Case in point: I was just about to lay my oars in the waters of Memory's Bliss, when we were rushed by a hip-hop icon, a figurehead, leading a crew of guys too built to be in the music business. One fist stole my microphone, another threw me from the stage. Punched me off the stage, at my own concert.

I haven't hit the ground yet.

This guy, he's considered a Teacher. That's what this is all about, some statements I made in an interview. I called his music sadistic. Said, "Rappers who are black, trying to prove manhood, make things worse. Make mountains out of molehills. Say nothing at all." But

The Teacher was most offended when I questioned what it was that he taught.

He'll try to justify his hypocrisy, stating, "I'm a teacher of respect." This act of aggression, from the same man who masterminded the "Stop the Violence" records, will set a precedent for copycats. His music is deafened by rage. And the so-called Teacher will spend many years trying to stop the reverberation.

Maybe my fans will catch me. Hold me up. Carry me gently back to the stage, embodying the peace and love and unity and fun crap they peddle. Maybe they'll denounce the fraud on stage, the Teacher demanding that they jump. But impact approaches. I can almost taste the sticky rum and coke floor. I don't know where my brother is. Maybe hiding under his turntable. Maybe wrapped around it. The Teacher, he just cut our beat off. Spandau Ballet hasn't been heard since.

Music groups die quicker than sound waves. Ex-fans let me fall — face first into obscurity. Maybe you'll dig me out of a record bin. Resuscitate me for reality television. Prop me up to audition for my own reenactment.

THE UNREMARKABLE

There are no scripts to inscribe them legendary, those who swallowed themselves. Those whose eyes lived atop their feet and whistles surrendered seats. They still had to report to work daily. School remained in session.

There are no holidays for those who opt against martyrdom. No PBS specials for cogs preceding the cotton gin. No commissioned tales about those who walked to work over Washington.

There are no miniseries, no relief aid, for the skin sacks hanging heavy, too swollen to recognize as human faces.

No dialogue coaches helping to craft. No speeches for those who lived in subtext. No sprawling stomp-and-shout musicals for the somber.

Those who hit the floor as bullets spit rage. Those under sheets, terrified of the thirsty teeth and all that water. Those courageous, brave enough to hide. Who peeled potatoes with gracious hum saved for meat and grain. Who withered, died of natural causes. Those who lived.

RESPONSE #2: THE COLOSSUS WEEPS

In April 2010, Arizona Governor Jan Brewer signed a bill allowing law enforcement to arrest individuals who fit the profile of a Mexican unable to produce documentation of U.S. citizenship. One month later, Governor Brewer signed another bill, this time authored by Schools Chief Tom Horne, to remove Ethnic Studies — specifically Mexican-American Studies — from Tucson schools in an effort to deter "ethnic solidarity." Soon, former Alaskan Governor Sarah Palin was on the scene, stating, "It's time for Americans across this great country to stand up and say, 'We're all Arizonans now.'"

My name's not Rodriguez; it's a fiber in the wind,
it's what oceans have immersed,
it's what's graceful and sublime over the top of peaks,
what grows red in desert sands.
—*Luis Rodriguez*

Tear down our mother of exiles. We have grown into a brazen giant whose conquering limbs, far flung, horde lands with starry pomp. Too aloof to recognize the parts of us ancient, we neglect that which is precious. Destroy, deny our selfhood with every lie.

But there is nothing erasure can conceal. There is no pundit able to slogan-slay the metaphysical. The truth is written in bone. The land's anatomy, its imperfect architecture, provides irrefutable depositions, slow erosion, buried teeth, treaties not worth the hemp printed upon, artifacts thought lost, spinal impressions. It's all there.

Colonist limbs paint murals of theoretical borders. A fence. Who has crossed the line in the sand? Kidnapping. Gunfire. Drug trade. Human trade. Whose appetite snorts the powder, smokes the weed, shoots the horse, consumes the body? Who acquires this mural, this sun burnt, white-knuckled traveling exhibit meant to justify things yet to come?

Things yet to come are all too familiar. Fractured history splinters the imagination into precedents without context. Thus inspired, the irrational revisionist wishes to change what is bone. What is in the flesh.

Any attempt to excavate criminal wrongdoings will be swiftly slandered. Treason! Paranoia! Unpatriotic!

Coded language meant to justify things yet to come.

Documentation first. Always first. Then the body: the look, the skin, the nose. Who is calloused, who is hungry? Next the mouth: the accent. What do their prayers sound like, to whom do they pray?

The New Colossus welcomed "fore fathers," only so that they could enlist in the great American pastime: re-imagining a future free of the Other. The mouth: nagging voices of the oppressed. Things yet to come. Erased fathers. Silenced mothers. Colonial aggression a cacophonous cloud, arms ascending over families brown, plucking one from another.

Now the children of these forgotten families seek to translate what has been tattooed inside of them. Driven to make sense of our collective history. Driven to reenact its theater in their minds. Who are the Americas? Who are the Arizonians? Their attempts to remember are human. Our attempts to annihilate are cannibalistic.

QUESTIONNAIRE FOR UNITED STATES/ INDONESIA STUDIES EXCHANGE

Where are your ancestors from?

Wherever they harvested luck. In the midst of the undocumented ash, there is one surviving fact of origin: my ancestors survived an inferno, a shade of evil my imagination fails to depict.

A Brief Chronology:

> My bloodline, surging somewhere within the 11.7 million square miles of the so-called Dark Continent.
>
> Horrified humans as import commodity, forced onto a rotting, rat-infested ship.
>
> Auction showcased in Maryland or Virginia.
>
> Chained to sprawling plantations in Georgia and Mississippi.
>
> Emancipation, then sharecropping, then Jim Crow.
>
> Pecans, peaches, chitlins, greens. Switches. Glaucoma. Pocketknives.
>
> Invented sur-names. Others, nameless. Tiptoed from master bedrooms to slave quarters, a legacy of rape revealed by the varied skin tones at my family reunion.
>
> Kidnapped. Humiliated. Tortured. Exploited. Traumatized. And they were the lucky ones.

What is your occupation?

Balancing wonder with adulthood. Performing magic, creating

distractions, changing everyday language into flowers. Dismantling (and rebuilding) familiar phrases. Obsessing over dead nouns, like freedom, justice, America, and race. Unraveling the lies woven into our nation's flag. I am occupied with absorbing forgotten landscapes and peoples, stealing information and then redistributing it. Touring the Heartland's community colleges, igniting ideas into discourse. And talking trash.

What are your hobbies?

Declaring to learn new things, then plopping into my comfy green recliner.

What are your favorite things about the United States, as a country?

We are one big mixed tape. A world beat set to hustle, to madness. Praise songs interwoven with lust.

Slang littering Academia. Complications, intersections, rough patches that file smooth slowly over time.

What are the things you dislike about the United States, as a country?

The nagging mule of white supremacy. The stench of factory-farmed cattle. Oh yeah, and Michael Bay Hollywood.

What do you know about Indonesia?

To be honest, Indonesia rarely crosses my mind. I'm sure that I've seen it on a map. Heard about it some during the 2008 election. Obama lived there, right? Perhaps you can confess the same narrow ignorance. I hope so. I hope that you are able to suppress the turmoil when the United States pollutes your politics, your airwaves. We feed on your terror. Live off your pleasure center. Please, save yourself: become a self-appointed expert on all things local. Reclaim Indonesia. Deconstruct what you know about the U.S.

In your opinion, do you think the United States is still a racist country?

I.

The one-drop rule is a colloquial term here in the US. It translates to the social classification as "black" of individuals with any African ancestry. The notion of invisible and/or intangible membership to a single racial group is uniquely applied to peoples of black African ancestry.

II.

Obama is the son of an immigrant African father and a white American mother. Yet on his 2010 census form, he marked "black" under the race category.

What do you think about the treatment of Muslims in the United States?

I am reminded of the beautifully shot, black and white, three and a half hour epic films depicting ghost pale families loaded in boxcars. Something rings familiar.

If you could change one thing about the United States, what would it be?

I would dismantle the public school system for 3 whole years. Place our children in apprenticeships while we re-imagine a scenario in which real learning can occur.

What is your favorite decade is US history, and why?

This current decade, no doubt. Why? Reference question number one.

A JUNGLE TALE

Little Black Sambo, Emmanuel Webster Lewis, and those two
dumbo Magpies skip the jungle floor, barefoot.

From the brush, a shottie cocks. High-pitched chuckle, "Huh-uh-
uh-uh-uh-uh-uh-uh." It's Elmer Fudd, double-barrel armed.

Little Black Sambo saunters up, shoots his finger into one of the
barrels. Elmer pulls trigger and the shottie explodes, his pumpkin
face now smeared with soot. Colored charcoal black he crumbles into
leaves and vines, bawling, bawling, "What do I do now?"

The Magpies croon. Slow, sad.

Webster and Little Black Sambo comfort Fudd. A gentle back and
forth, forth and back, until Fudd's tears dry salt. Then Webster and
Little Black Sambo join the Magpies in a soulful rendition of Ol'
Man River.

With bright, demon red lipstick, they circle Fudd's mouth one-two-
three times. Hoist him in the air.

Their song rising and rising until it reaches rousing:

He just keeps rolling
He keeps on rolling
Along

From the treetops they wail and belt. The magpies flap to keep beat.
The jungle itself is now caught in the toxic sway.

Tote that barge
Lift that bale

You gets a little drunk
and you land in jail

The monkeys clasp their tales in chain. The elephants link their trunks. The warthogs lock their tiny tusks in unison. All manner of wild creature join:

But Ol' Man River
        He just keeps rolling
                Along

Except the tiger, of course. The tiger who lurks, watching. Low in the brush. Statue silent. Going to eat these cherubs. Eat them as soon as they come down from the trees. As soon as the music stops.

WHEN BLACK ACTORS WIN OSCARS

When black actors win Oscars, it sounds like this:

Thank you, Academy. It's been a journey. I started as a mugger/ rapist in a Dirty Harry film. Since then, my path has been paved with pimps, jesters, street hustlers, jive talking–con men. Needless to say, when I read Alfred's script, I jumped at the chance. I mean, when else does one get the opportunity drive the legendary Jessica Tandy around Georgia.

It sounds like this:

This is for you Sydney! Sydney, I been chasing you for years. Sydney, you were the model. It was you Sydney, it was you. You were our caped crusader. Our Jackie Robinson. Sydney. Sydney. Sydney.

Like this:

First, I should thank my agents. You were right about the polarities guys. I admit, I thought for sure I'd win for X. For sure Biko. For sure The Martyr. But you were right, play the polarities. Last year I won as the virginal eunuch messiah who helped those poor German nuns. And this year, this year I win as the savage gangster cop. God bless you all.

Like this:

I knew I was a shoe in. Who doesn't love a blind, drug-addicted blues man who abandons the gospel for mainstream success?

Like this:

This is a shock. I am shocked. Ben Kinglsey as the Indian. Charlton Heston as the Mexican. Sacha Baron Cohen as the Arab. Joleson and Downey under masks of charcoal. Who could compete? I thought

I had no chance. Thankfully, a dictatorial murderer of Africans was the role I was born to play.

Like this:

This is for all of the actors before me, who suffered through humiliating roles as coons and servants. This Oscar goes to the bojangles, the fetchits, the remus'. I could feel their spirits on set. They lent me the strength to play this long-suffering slave, this sage with ample advice for his young white co-star.

When black actors win Oscars its sounds like:

I love you! I love you all. Thank you. Thank you. I love you. I love you. Thank you! I love you all. Thanks. I don't deserve this. I don't. I don't deserve you.

And:

It was my wonderful Australian co-signer. I mean, co-star.

And:

This Oscar is for my grandmother. She was my first acting teacher. She'd say act like you been somewhere. Act like you got some sense. And when I would act out she'd applaud my performance with a beating. Grandma always told me to act like I got some sense. Too bad I make more money when I don't.

I wait for the day it will sound like this:

In this business, we manufacture dreams, yearnings. We embody the vast collective hopes. That's easier than railroads and automobiles. But this Oscar goes to the African American dreams that aren't coming to any theater near you.

THE NAT TURNER CHASE MOVIE PITCH

So Nat Turner — word — so Nat Turner — word up, word up, you with me? — so Nat Turner, he's straight up runnin', like Run Lola Run sprinting through that, um, that, um, that desert, alright? Yeah, like Arizona stretch. He in Death Valley. Word. Word. So, so, so. Sweat pourin' down his blue black — ok? — his blue black, that blue black. Nappy ass skull, ok?

This is Nat Turner, riiiigghht? Still got his hand on that axe-hatchet, ok? That axe-hatchet, ok? So Nat runnin'. Tattered shirt and pants. Got holy books tied to his feet on some sacrilege. At this point he blown holes across the road.

It's a road joint, like blacktop duel or duel or blacktop asphalt cowboy, a joint like Easy Rider, or the joint with Geena Davis and the convertible.

Nat Turner along the desert, runnin' on those books like I mentioned, and Nat bein' followed. He bein' followed. From miles around they heard how much he spilled. When they reach him, they gon crack his bones. They gon suck out that marrow.

So, word. So, word.

It's blazing before the eclipse. Once it eclipse, he fall. And when he fall, the coyotes, they start talkin'. Rattlesnakes, they start talkin'. And he get to likin' the sound, ok? The shake of that viper, it coaxes it up out of him, ok?

Cold arid desert keep him curled up. And the coyotes they talkin', and the rattlesnakes they talkin'. And Nat, he listening to the predators. The predators is talkin' and the prey, they hidin'. The jackrabbit is hidin'. The tortoise too, ok? They all curled up in holes. Gon underground. But Nat? My man Nat? Big bloody Nat?

Handsome black hat Nat? He's in that desert just listenin'. Catchin' that breath, takin' in a lesson, ok? Learnin' that lesson. Free advice from those that roam with too big a presence to be caught. They hold court.

And when that eclipse pass – the eclipse, it slips back into the blistering heat, cakin' that dried up blood on that weapon like I said – that's when Nat get back to runnin', riiiiight?

He ride. But they wont catch him.

Even after they do — cuz they do catch him — it aint him. Cuz out there in that eclipse, he passed it to the rattlesnake. Passed it to the coyote. Blew across that crispy desert sand.

That boy and his cold stare, that beating chest, he like a vision of the future. He gon run.

Helicopters choppin' the sky on some Michael Bay. The tractor beam warmin' up like satellites on some Stanley Kurbick, ya heard?

They gon catch him. Word. I know, I know, I know. Word. I know. But before they kill 'em — we all know that — the moment before, we gon cut. We smash gon cut. No fade out slow. Just black. Sharp like lightening.

They caught 'em, but it aint him. Cuz out there in that eclipse, he passed it to the rattlesnake. Passed it to the coyote. Blew across that crispy desert sand.

ON TOUR WITH THE KING

The true revolutionary is guided by a great feeling of love.
— Che Guevara

You'll go mad trying to mute the rhythm of pawn shop, storefront church, parking lot, fast food joint. When you visit Detroit, Malik will gracefully navigate the side streets strewn with peeling paint. He'll merge on and off the endless highways. Wind and zip knowingly through vacant neighborhoods, pointing out the phantom architecture.

You look through the window at the acne scarred granite face with teeth missing. Identical to the last dozen you've driven past. You sigh but Malik is a loop of what was once and what's to be. Cultural centers. New business districts. An improved waterfront. He confirms what you've been hearing about the urban farms and the national news swarming about like sensational buzzards. Malik speaks a blinding future of progress. He conjures posters in the Thomas Edison Museum, the nuclear family in their Sunday bests, just home from a drive in the Chevrolet.

Malik is paying his debt to the land he knows better than his own face. He works long weeks to change the rhythm. He mutes the cacophony of blight, singles out the sparkling bells, brings up the volume on the thumping pulse. He is Clyde Stubblefield, keeping the beat steady hoping to lure the city's James Brown emotion into his groove.

Many children of the city stay tuned to Detroit's frequency. They are naive enough to see utopia and loud enough to demand its birth. When you visit Detroit you'll go mad unless you're looking through their eyes.

You shouldn't see it any other way.

ACKNOWLEDGEMENTS:

There are countless meaningful interactions, from Sept. 26 1977 through May. 2010, that inspired and/or deeply informed the creation of this book. I can't possibly name everyone or everything but I will say that I did not do any of this alone. I am truly blessed in immeasurable ways!

I must however give a few special acknowledgements pertaining specifically to the creation of *These Are The Breaks*.

> Much love and appreciation to Felicia Rose Chavez for carefully helping me shape this into something worth reading. *I couldn't have done it without you* doesn't begin to sum up my level of gratitude.

> Tall Godzilla props are in order for my comrade Kevin Coval for his invaluable insights, encouragement and ears.

> 'Nuff respect to the publisher and editors for all of their sweat and faith that I too could get busy on the page.

> Extra special thanks to Brett Neiman for designing the hell out my cover.

Also, it should be noted that a variation of "Old Ladies and Dope Boys" appeared in the August 2008 issue of *Lunarosity*.

"Something About Lying" was commissioned for *Teacher Tales*, part of the Steppenwolf Theater's *Traffic* Reading Series. So a special thanks to my pal Dr. Robert S Boone for inviting me.

Early versions of "The Headbanger," "The Gangster Rap Question," "10 Up," and "Esham" were written and performed as artist in residence on KRUI Iowa's *Artists In Action* Radio Program. So special thanks to Martin, Jen and Sean for letting me infect the listeners of Iowa City.

Super extra bionic computer love to you reader! If you liked it, tell a friend, loan it out, talk or tweet or text or twizzle twazzle[14] about it. We keep it grassroots 'round here and there are no small gestures.

And I'm out...

Idris Goodwin

---

14   I made this word up.

ABOUT THE AUTHOR

IDRIS GOODWIN is an NEA award-winning playwright, break beat poet, indie rapper and teacher. His work examines the intersection of personal truth and political absurdity. Both his stage-plays and solo performances are enjoyed by diverse audiences across the nation. He has been featured on HBO's *Def Poetry* and The Discovery Channel's *Planet Green*. His latest album, *Break Beat Poems*, earned praise from *The New York Times* and National Public Radio. As an educator, Idris promotes cross-cultural literacy at colleges, K-12 schools, and community organizations.

WWW.IDRISGOODWIN.BLOGSPOT.COM

WB 2011 LINEUP

38 BAR BLUES
A collection of poems by C.R .Avery

WORKIN' MIME TO FIVE
Humor by Derrick Brown

YESTERDAY WON'T GOODBYE
New poems by Brian Ellis

THESE ARE THE BREAKS
New prose & poetry by Idris Goodwin

THE FEATHER ROOM
New poems by Anis Mojgani

LOVE IN A TIME OF ROBOT APOCALYPSE
New poems by David Perez

THE UNDISPUTED GREATEST WRITER OF ALL TIME
New poems by Beau Sia

SUNSET AT THE TEMPLE OF OLIVES
New poems by Paul Suntup

GENTLEMAN PRACTICE
New poems by Buddy Wakefield

HOW TO SEDUCE A WHITE BOY IN TEN EASY STEPS
New poems by Laura Yes Yes

THE NEW CLEAN
New poems by Jon Sands

BRING DOWN THE CHANDELIERS
New poems by Tara Hardy

WRITE ABOUT AN EMPTY BIRDCAGE
New poems by Elaina M. Ellis

REASONS TO LEAVE THE SLAUGHTER
New poems by Ben Clark

OTHER WRITE BLOODY BOOKS

EVERYTHING IS EVERYTHING (2010)
New poems by Cristin O'Keefe Aptowicz

DEAR FUTURE BOYFRIEND (2010)
A Write Bloody reissue of Cristin O'Keefe Aptowicz's first book of poetry

HOT TEEN SLUT (2010)
A Write Bloody reissue of Cristin O'Keefe Aptowicz's second book of poetry
about her time writing for porn

WORKING CLASS REPRESENT (2010)
A Write Bloody reissue of Cristin O'Keefe Aptowicz's third book of poetry

OH, TERRIBLE YOUTH (2010)
A Write Bloody reissue of Cristin O'Keefe Aptowicz's fourth book of poetry
about her terrible youth

CATACOMB CONFETTI (2010)
New poems by Josh Boyd

THE BONES BELOW (2010)
New poems by Sierra DeMulder

CEREMONY FOR THE CHOKING GHOST (2010)
New poems by Karen Finneyfrock

MILES OF HALLELUJAH (2010)
New poems by Rob "Ratpack Slim" Sturma

RACING HUMMINGBIRDS (2010)
New poems by Jeanann Verlee

YOU BELONG EVERYWHERE (2010)
Road memoir and how-to guide for travelling artists

LEARN THEN BURN (2010)
Anthology of poems for the classroom. Edited by Tim Stafford and Derrick Brown.

STEVE ABEE, GREAT BALLS OF FLOWERS (2009)
New poems by Steve Abee

SCANDALABRA (2009)
New poetry compilation by Derrick Brown

DON'T SMELL THE FLOSS (2009)
New Short Fiction Pieces By Matty Byloos

THE LAST TIME AS WE ARE (2009)
New poems by Taylor Mali

IN SEARCH OF MIDNIGHT: THE MIKE MCGEE HANDBOOK OF AWESOME (2009)
New poems by Mike McGee

ANIMAL BALLISTICS (2009)
New poems by Sarah Morgan

CAST YOUR EYES LIKE RIVERSTONES INTO THE EXQUISITE DARK (2009)
New poems by Danny Sherrard

SPIKING THE SUCKER PUNCH (2009)
New poems by Robbie Q. Telfer

THE GOOD THINGS ABOUT AMERICA (2009)
An illustrated, un-cynical look at our American Landscape. Various authors.
Edited by Kevin Staniec and Derrick Brown

THE ELEPHANT ENGINE HIGH DIVE REVIVAL (2009)
Anthology

THE CONSTANT VELOCITY OF TRAINS (2008)
New poems by Lea C. Deschenes

HEAVY LEAD BIRDSONG (2008)
New poems by Ryler Dustin

UNCONTROLLED EXPERIMENTS IN FREEDOM (2008)
New poems by Brian Ellis

POLE DANCING TO GOSPEL HYMNS (2008)
Poems by Andrea Gibson

CITY OF INSOMNIA (2008)
New poems by Victor D. Infante

WHAT IT IS, WHAT IT IS (2008)
Graphic Art Prose Concept book by Maust of Cold War Kids and author Paul Maziar

OVER THE ANVIL WE STRETCH (2008)
New poems by Anis Mojgani

NO MORE POEMS ABOUT THE MOON (2008)
NON-Moon poems by Michael Roberts

JUNKYARD GHOST REVIVAL (2008)
with Andrea Gibson, Buddy Wakefield, Anis Mojgani, Derrick Brown, Robbie Q,
Sonya Renee and Cristin O'Keefe Aptowicz

THE LAST AMERICAN VALENTINE:
ILLUSTRATED POEMS TO SEDUCE AND DESTROY (2008)
24 authors, 12 illustrators team up for a collection of non-sappy love poetry.
Edited by Derrick Brown

LETTING MYSELF GO (2007)
Bizarre god comedy & wild prose by Buzzy Enniss

LIVE FOR A LIVING (2007)
New poems by Buddy Wakefield

SOLOMON SPARROWS ELECTRIC WHALE REVIVAL (2007)
Poetry compilation by Buddy Wakefield, Anis Mojgani, Derrick Brown, Dan
Leamen & Mike McGee

I LOVE YOU IS BACK (2006)
Poetry compilation (2004-2006) by Derrick Brown

BORN IN THE YEAR OF THE BUTTERFLY KNIFE (2004)
Poetry anthology, 1994-2004 by Derrick Brown

SOME THEY CAN'T CONTAIN (2004)
Classic poetry compilation by Buddy Wakefield

WRITEBLOODY
QUALITY AMERICAN BOOKS

WWW.WRITEBLOODY.COM

WRITEBLOODY
QUALITY AMERICAN BOOKS

PULL YOUR BOOKS UP BY THEIR BOOTSTRAPS

Write Bloody Publishing distributes and promotes great books of fiction, poetry and art every year. We are an independent press dedicated to quality literature and book design, with an office in Long Beach, CA.

Our employees are authors and artists so we call ourselves a family. Our design team comes from all over America: modern painters, photographers and rock album designers create book covers we're proud to be judged by.

We publish and promote 8-12 tour-savvy authors per year. We are grass-roots, D.I.Y., bootstrap believers. Pull up a good book and join the family. Support independent authors, artists and presses.

Visit us online:

WRITEBLOODY.COM

CPSIA information can be obtained at www.ICGtesting.com
Printed in the USA
BVOW07s1936291014

372898BV00002B/10/P